I'M SUPPOSED TO BE DOING THIS

I'M SUPPOSED TO BE DOING THIS

AN ADULT GAP YEAR

SUZANNE ROSKE

NEW DEGREE PRESS
COPYRIGHT © 2023 SUZANNE ROSKE
All rights reserved.

I'M SUPPOSED TO BE DOING THIS
An Adult Gap Year

ISBN   979-8-88504-459-2 *Paperback*
        979-8-88504-483-7 *Ebook*

For Bill, Emily, Zane, and Quinn. You are my heart and the reason I'm supposed to be doing this. Thank you for going on this adventure with me.

CONTENTS

INTRODUCTION — 11

CHAPTER 1. MY BIG IDEA — 21
CHAPTER 2. BURNOUT — 27
CHAPTER 3. THE MAIL — 35
CHAPTER 4. EXPLANATIONS — 39
CHAPTER 5. FAMILIES STAY TOGETHER — 47
CHAPTER 6. ARRIVAL — 53
CHAPTER 7. TEAM COLORADO — 61
CHAPTER 8. GOLDEN THREADS — 69
CHAPTER 9. SILENCE — 79
CHAPTER 10. MAGGOTS — 87
CHAPTER 11. PIÑATAS — 91
CHAPTER 12. THE GODDESS WITHIN — 97
CHAPTER 13. FAMILY VALUES — 103
CHAPTER 14. FAILURE — 109
CHAPTER 15. ESMERALDA — 115
CHAPTER 16. THE WHITE BOARD — 121
CHAPTER 17. ASKING FOR HELP — 125
CHAPTER 18. IDENTITY — 133
CHAPTER 19. STUFF — 141
CHAPTER 20. HUMMINGBIRD — 149
CHAPTER 21. DELFINES — 157

CHAPTER 22. PUMPKIN SEEDS   165
CHAPTER 23. WHAT'S YOUR PLAN?   175
CHAPTER 24. BITTERSWEET   189

EPILOGUE   195
ACKNOWLEDGMENTS   199
APPENDIX   205

*Almost everything will work
if you unplug it for a few minutes...
including you.*

—ANNE LAMOTT

INTRODUCTION

It's never too late to be what you might have been.
—GEORGE ELIOT

On July 14, 2020, a seemingly uneventful day in the sameness of COVID, I received the email announcement I knew was coming but somehow still wasn't prepared for. My children, like most others around the world, would not return to in-person school in the fall. Until that email, I held onto a glimmer of hope school would return some degree of normalcy to our lives. A wish, perhaps, that what I hadn't been able to give my kids during the first months of the pandemic—time, attention, interaction—school would provide. Once again, COVID broke my spirit.

As I pondered the implications of the school's announcement, the small voice inside my head whispered, *Is this really what I'm supposed to be doing?*

For as long as I could remember, I was the one who had it under control. I knew what I wanted and would go get it. I learned the rules of the game early. It was a donut-eating contest, and I was out to win. Over the years, I'd honed my craft. I won the contests only to discover the prize for winning was more donuts. After years of eating donuts, I realized I was tired of them. But I had no idea what else I could eat or what I even liked. The truth was I was too scared, or maybe just too comfortable, to do anything about it.

On that Tuesday in July, the small voice that had been restless for so long—only to be squashed by my internal drive and the notion that I *had it all* so who was I to complain—finally shouted at the top of her lungs...

You are not happy! You can do better! You must do better!

Unfortunately, at that moment, I had no idea what "better" could possibly look like. I had worked so long and so hard. From the outside looking in, I had it all.

THE GREAT RESIGNATION OR THE GREAT REPRIORITIZATION

It has been dubbed the "Great Resignation" (Kellett 2022). Spurred by the COVID-19 pandemic, over forty-seven million Americans voluntarily left their jobs in 2021 (SHRM 2022). These numbers represented an unprecedented follow-on to the resignation numbers experienced in 2020, the first year of the pandemic. And although the country has seen the recovery of jobs across industries, most sustained pandemic-related job losses have been experienced by women (Ewing-Nelson 2021). According to a report from the National Women's Law Center, from February 2020 to December 2020, women in the United States accounted for 5.4 million net job losses, significantly outpacing net job losses experienced by men during the same period (Ewing-Nelson 2021).

I was one of them.

American workers left the workforce in 2020 and 2021 for numerous reasons. Certainly, people were forced to leave their jobs when their positions were eliminated early in the pandemic. But even as the economy recovered, employees continued to leave the workforce at record numbers. Employees were reconsidering what was important to them and how they could find fulfillment during a time when so many things were beyond their control.

For many people, including myself, the reflection and reprioritization went beyond wrestling with increased responsibilities on the home front. We were forced to listen to the small voice inside that had been wondering, *Is this what I am supposed to be doing?*

How does one begin to answer that question? When I was growing up in the late 1980s and early 1990s, the stereotypical response to the question "Is this all there is?" was the mid-life crisis; buy a sports car, get breast or hair implants, have an affair with a younger man or woman. Those options not only seemed outdated and trite in the present day, but they also went against my moral compass, and frankly seemed exhausting.

In her book *The Gifts of Imperfection,* Dr. Brené Brown reframes the midlife crisis as a *midlife unraveling.* "A time when you feel a desperate pull to live the life you want to live, not the one you're 'supposed' to live. The unraveling is a time when you are challenged by the universe to let go of who you think you are supposed to be and embrace who you are" (Brown 2020, xxvi).

"Midlife is when the universe gently places her hands upon your shoulders, pulls you close, and whispers in your ear: 'I'm not screwing around. All of this pretending and performing…has to go. …Time is growing short. There are unexplored adventures ahead of you. …It's time to show up and be seen'" (Brown 2018).

Now, this definition was closer to what I was experiencing—not the 1980s notion of running away from who I was, but the more refined and authentic approach of running to whom I was meant to be.

The question of *how* remained. I knew I couldn't do it where I was, on the career treadmill that was going ever faster each year. Like Scooby Doo, my legs were moving fast, but I wasn't getting anywhere. I had to step off and step away.

AN ADULT GAP YEAR

"Suzanne, you are eight years old and that's old enough to have a job. This summer, when you aren't in swimming classes or art lessons, you will work at the family hardware store," my Pop-Pop Spike said in 1983.

This was my introduction to the working world. I have been working ever since. I worked at my family's store every summer from the time I was eight until I was twenty-one. My nickname in college was even Suzi-TruValue. And although I loved working with my family, I never had a doubt in my mind I wanted a career outside of the store. Something in the city. Something in an office building. Something where I'd wear a suit and have to commute. *Seriously, I wanted to sit in traffic!* The path ahead of me was college and then a corporate job. I never considered anything else. I wish I could go back and shake some sense into twenty-one-year-old me.

In the mid-1990s, taking a gap year between high school and college was not common in the United States. People like me jumped straight from high school to college or college to work without a second thought. Today, however, the number of students taking a gap year has increased significantly with almost 40 percent of students considering a gap year (Horn 2020). The gap year has been reframed as a "Year on Purpose" where the main goals are to learn about yourself, your strengths, your purpose, and what pathways are available to you (Horn 2020).

So what happens when what you wanted, or thought you wanted at twenty-one, isn't what you want at forty-five? How does someone go about finding themselves?

If I had been younger, I would have embraced the notion of a gap year. Exploring the world with a backpack and a curious eye for adventure.

If I had been single, I could have left everything behind *Eat, Pray, Love* style (Gilbert 2006).

If I wasn't so far up the career ladder, I could have stepped away without fear others would take my position and I would become irrelevant.

If I were older, I'd figure out what was next as part of my retirement plan.

But I wasn't any of these things. I was a forty-five-year-old wife, a mother of three, and a partner at a management consulting firm. I had responsibilities.

Conventional wisdom says you don't walk away from the career you have built over twenty-five years to find what you are supposed to be doing. You find a way to muscle through. You appreciate the material things and status you have accumulated. You take a vacation, try to put the computer down, and take pleasure in a break. You put aside the notion of finding yourself and move on because finding yourself could mean losing everything you have worked for.

But what if you could step away, and who says gap years are reserved for the young?

When I hit my breaking point, I needed all the benefits that could come from a gap year, reflecting on who I was and how I could best contribute to the world. I just happened to be significantly older than the eighteen-to-twenty-two-year-old age demographic typically associated with a gap year.

And who says you must wait for retirement to figure out what's next? I wasn't ready to stop working. But I needed to figure out what I was supposed to be doing.

I believe a mid-career break or an "adult gap year" can be transformative. Why do I say that?

Because I took an adult gap year.

When faced with the unavoidable truth I wasn't happy and I could do better for myself and my family, I stepped away. Not just away into the confines of quarantine, but away to Oaxaca, Mexico. And yes, my family came with me.

When viewed with a mindset of abundance rather than scarcity, an adult gap year presents opportunities that can propel you forward, leading you to what you are supposed to be doing. When you slow down, you have the opportunity to reconnect with who you are and what you truly value. When you have the courage to let go of the expectations, of both you and others, you can find freedom and happiness. I believe if you want to be someone other than who you are right now, whether you seek a slight change or a major overhaul, you must be willing to take a risk. You must be willing to unlearn and relearn.

An adult gap year is not a vacation or an escape. You will dismantle the person you have created, the one you thought you were supposed to be, the one others see you as. You may expose dark secrets and truths about yourself that are sometimes easier left unseen. It is a hell of a lot of work. But it can be done. You are investing in yourself. You are creating a future where you will live into your values. You are figuring out what you're supposed to be doing, on your terms.

You don't need to run off to a foreign locale to have an adult gap year—although if you have the means, I highly recommend it, as it was the best thing I have ever done. But you do need to commit the time and create the space for introspection, learning and unlearning, and self-renewal. You need to slow down long enough so you can hear yourself and find the leader who lies within you and whom you want to be. You need to connect to *that* person.

WARNING—CHANGE AWAITS YOU
This book will not teach you how to plan or execute an adult gap year. Trust me, you don't want me to be your guide. We architected our family's Mexican adventure in two weeks and just went with it. I had no idea what we were getting ourselves into, and I felt freedom in the naivete of not knowing. If I had known more, I'm sure I would have backed out in fear of all the complexities I couldn't anticipate.

This book is my story of how I got to the point where I knew something had to change. I needed to step off the corporate treadmill because I could do better, yet I had no idea where to start. It is my story of feeling aimless and without a guide as I searched for what was next. It is my story of the lessons I learned and relearned about connecting to my family and living my values. This is my story of listening to the leader within me so I could figure out what I am supposed to be doing.

If I had stayed put in my life as I had known it, sure I would have made it and likely been fine. But I would have missed out on so much, like finding freedom in dancing by the Pacific Ocean during a yoga retreat; rediscovering the simple blessings of family and the pride of hard work while buying a Christmas *piñata*; creating family memories I will cherish forever; and above all, getting to know myself again.

As I sit here today writing this book, I hope if you are trying to figure out what you're supposed to be doing or are considering an adult gap year, you will find meaning, inspiration, and a few laughs in my stories and the lessons I relearned. Namely, you can find value in slowing down and freedom in letting go; you are a hell of a lot stronger than you think you are; and if you listen carefully to your heart and the universe, you will find your path forward—even when it is hard. Oh, and there likely will be maggots.

CHAPTER ONE

MY BIG IDEA

Everything begins with an idea.
—EARL NIGHTINGALE

"I have a crazy idea. What if we moved to Mexico this year? The kids can Zoom into remote school. You've always worked remotely so it shouldn't matter where you work. I can take a sabbatical. We can turn COVID into an adventure," I proposed to my husband Bill as we ate dinner on the screened porch of the cabin we were renting.

The summer sun slowly sank behind the Appalachian Mountains of North Carolina, the buzz of cicadas grew louder, and the breeze gently attempted to usher out the heat as dusk settled around us. Everything seemed to be moving in three-quarters time. Bill looked at me with equal parts confusion and curiosity, considering my idea. I had no idea what he was thinking, but my proposal was out there. Now I waited.

I felt like everything was hanging on Bill's response. In the few hours since it occurred to me we could live out COVID's quarantine almost anywhere, my idea transformed from merely a possibility into a calling. Not a choice, really, but the only logical path forward. You see, I lost myself long ago—lost myself in my work and the roles I had assumed: a consulting firm partner, mother, compliance expert, locator of lost things, wife, process improvement guru, interior designer and project architect, business integration leader, comfort provider, workforce and change management sage, friend, chauffeur, chef, COO of the home, teacher, keeper of the schedule, and an occasional drill sergeant, among other things. I was a lot of things to many people, yet I had no idea who I was or what I wanted.

As a relative problem in the world, the fact I was "lost" was minor. By most objective measures I was successful and had "made it." People across the world suffered on a scale far greater than me, a scale I generally couldn't comprehend. I recognized my privilege. Who was I to complain? Like a good overachiever when thoughts such as, *Am I really supposed to be doing this?* or *Is this all there is?* surfaced, I pushed my feelings down and ignored them. Until I couldn't anymore.

On July 14, 2020, I received an email, and with that "ping" my moment of reckoning arrived. My children, like most children around the world, would not return to in-person school in the fall. Logically, this announcement was coming, but I still wasn't ready for it. *Arlington Public Schools will make every attempt to return your children to the classroom as soon as it is safe.* In my heart, I knew we were in for the long haul. I was crestfallen.

The experience and my emotions during the first few months of the pandemic had been all over the place.

Frustration.

Conference calls all day, every day. My kids had so little interaction with any adults, including me. I felt helpless. One morning I watched from another room, as Quinn slid out of her desk chair onto the floor where she stayed, staring at the ceiling for at least an hour. I didn't have time to help her. I was too busy helping businesses navigate the impact of COVID to even check on my child.

Rage.

Broadly directed at the pandemic for everything and everyone lost. More specifically directed at people's response to the situation.

"Why do you need to have dinner with your family? You've been home all day together," a male colleague demanded when I declined a 7 p.m. conference call so I could have dinner with my kids and husband.

And rage directed at me when I ultimately acquiesced to the call. I spent a few minutes at the dinner table before jumping back online because I didn't want people to think my work wasn't my number one priority.

Guilt and sadness.

Emily and Zane were struggling to navigate the normal challenges of being thirteen while dealing with the pandemic. It was brutal. They slammed doors, got lost in their devices, and seemed to withdraw into themselves a little more every day. I had no idea how to connect with them.

Unease.

"You are on the phone all day," Bill said. "All I hear is your voice." Bill had worked from home for years, so the shift to remote work was not new for him. But he typically had the house to himself during the day. It was clear he felt smothered by his new officemates. *Would our marriage and family survive all this togetherness?*

Amazement.

Before the pandemic, I went to the office or traveled frequently. I assumed we were doing fine and our house would be standing at the end of the day. But as I sat at home and watched life unfold around me, it seemed like our house and my family were held together with bubble gum and duct tape. I was amazed we didn't spontaneously combust multiple times throughout the day.

Stress.

It was unrelenting—the job, the expectations, the unknown, the next revenue target, the feelings of inadequacy, and the constant need to run faster, but despite trying really hard feeling like I never got anywhere.

I couldn't do it anymore.

COVID wasn't the cause of my discontent, but it certainly was the straw that broke the camel's back. For several years, I had noticed my small, internal voice asking, *Is this all there is?* and *Am I really supposed to be doing this?* Every time I felt this restlessness, my internal drive and the belief I had it all silenced the voice. *Who was I to complain?*

But COVID broke down my bravado because nothing was all right. My small voice finally shouted at the top of her lungs, *You are not happy. You can do better. You must do better.* Unfortunately, I had no idea what better could look like, so I went for a walk to clear my head.

Have you ever had a moment when the pieces come together, the fog lifts, and you suddenly see a possible way forward? As I walked up a steep dirt path, the sounds of my breath echoing in my ears and rumbling thunder in the distance, the pieces of a puzzle started coming together.

My kids were struggling. Even though they were older they seemed to need me more now than they did when they were little.

I was not intentionally directing my career; I was reacting. If I wanted to figure out what was next for me, I needed to step away from the day-to-day grind.

Bill and I had wanted to do a long-term international experience for more than fifteen years, but the timing had never been right. Maybe this was it—a unique moment in time.

Mexico. What if we moved to Mexico? Maybe, just maybe, we could take advantage of COVID. We could turn the lemons of a global pandemic into lemonade, or more appropriately said, turn limes into margaritas.

I ran (okay, fast-walked) back to the cabin. Excited and energized by the possibilities of my idea. I'll admit my plan was not well thought through when I presented it to Bill. I hadn't prepared my typical pro-con list, hadn't researched the feasibility of moving to a foreign country during a global quarantine, and—oh my god—what about the logistics? I'd think about that later. All I knew was this idea consumed me and if Bill was on board, we'd figure out a way to make it happen.

Bill considered my proposal for mere seconds, but it felt like an eternity. He looked at me like I had lost my mind. I felt heat rising in my body as the blood rushed to my face, embarrassed I thought my idea would work. Perhaps I was grasping at straws.

"Never mind," I said, as I quietly lowered my head in defeat. "It's a crazy idea. Forget about it."

Bill stopped me. He smiled. "Yes, it is a *crazy* idea. You're *crazy*. And we're doing this."

CHAPTER TWO

BURNOUT

You can have it all, just not it all at once.
—OPRAH WINFREY

Gold stars, stickers, letter grades, rankings at work. I have always been motivated by external rewards. In kindergarten, my class was separated into reading groups based on each student's ability. The Blue Birds were the best. But I was a Red Bird, which was not acceptable to my five-year-old self. I wanted to be a Blue Bird. According to my mother, I started reading all the time—Dr. Seuss, *Dick and Jane*, anything I could get my hands on. Unfortunately, I wasn't reading for the joy of reading. I was reading so I could become a Blue Bird. So prominent was my desire my teacher called a parent-teacher conference to reprimand my parents for *pushing* me to be in the *best group*.

"We aren't pressuring her. This is how Suzanne is wired. She is performing for your system. Show her a carrot, and she will not stop until she gets the carrot," my mother said in response to my teacher's attempted parenting lesson.

My internal wiring set me up for success in school and later as a management consultant. Over and over, I was shown the carrot, the brass ring, the donut—pick your metaphor. And over and over, I stretched and achieved the rewards. I would tell people, "Give me a checklist of what you need me to do, and I will tick off every box. Plus, I'll give you a little more for good measure."

The biggest carrot in front of me professionally was to be admitted to the partnership at my firm. With Bill's full support and a required move across the country, I decided that is what I wanted, and we decided to go for it. To be part of the partnership, an owner in the business. Although it took a few years, I eventually achieved my goal, but not without a lot of stress and sacrifice.

In August 2013, I received an email welcoming me to the partner admission process. I distinctly recall the sound of a starting gun going off in my head. I was in for a year-long sprint. From that moment on, my every move would be evaluated and scrutinized. Well-meaning mentors and advisors provided checklists to help me succeed: grow my business, keep my current clients happy, develop my team, manage up, find my voice but keep to the party lines, and literally the worst advice I've ever been given: "don't fuck it up." But I had a checklist and a really big carrot on the line. I could do this. All I had to do was work the list, keep it together, and never let them see me sweat.

On the surface, I lived up to expectations and ticked off every box put before me. I donned the mask that showed the poised, successful, and confident professional they wanted to see. I had it all together. I fit the mold. I emulated the other members of the club. I was shiny and bright for all to see. I kept the carrot in sight and worked toward that. The partnership was my goal. It was what I had worked for. Making partner would show others I had made it.

Underneath, however, I was profusely sweating. Wearing a mask and being someone who others wanted me to be was hard. The mask got heavy. On a Sunday evening in February, my mask cracked.

The triggering event was innocuous enough. Bill was out of town, and I was trying to wrangle three kids under the age of seven. Toys were out of place. Small humans with big personalities, fueled by sugar from ice cream sundaes, weren't interested in going to bed. The house was messy, which was outward evidence I couldn't keep it together. Honestly, I can't remember exactly what caused me to crack. But I exploded, releasing the overwhelming storm that had been building inside me for months.

"Zane, you need to clean up now! Stop dancing around and come here! Pick up your toys or I will throw your firetruck away. *Damn it! Do it now, Zane!*" I threatened. His firetruck was his favorite. I was loud, slamming pots and pans in the kitchen. I scared the kids and scared myself.

The rage in my voice was driven by my fear and my desire to control everything, but it had been directed at a small boy. Zane, in his footie pajamas with chocolate ice cream smeared across his face, looked up at me. His big blue eyes were filled with tears, but he wasn't crying. He stared at me with a look of shock and confusion, like I was a stranger.

Without a word of apology or comfort to Zane, I retreated to my bedroom. At once I felt shaken and ashamed of my outburst, but also a strange relief from finally releasing some of the emotions that had been bottled up within. I looked at myself in the mirror.

Who are you? Staring back was a woman without a mask. I barely recognized her. Her skin was gray. Her eyes were rimmed with dark circles.

What have you become? She was exhausted. She was stripped down to her core.

This wasn't the person I wanted to be, nor how I wanted to act. I liked very little about this person. I needed a break, but my race wasn't over. I had to keep going. I had no other choice. My head dropped, and I exhaled. And then another thought surfaced. It seemed to come from outside of me, as if someone else planted it in my brain: *What would it feel like to have a gun in my mouth?*

I was terrified by this thought. *Why would I think such a thing?* Shaking, heart racing, cold sweat running down my temples, I locked eyes with myself in the mirror. *Get yourself together, Suzanne.* I took a few deep breaths to steady myself. I knew what I needed to do. I picked up the mask and put it back on. It was a little heavier than before. A little shinier with a new coat of shellac. I walked out of my bedroom with a smile on my face.

I didn't tell anyone I had thought about putting a gun in my mouth on a Sunday evening in February 2014. Not my husband, not my colleagues, not my friends. I received professional help from a therapist, but I couldn't tell anyone else. I was so close to my goal. I just had to tick a few more boxes, smile, and project competence.

"Your stress responders are significantly weakened, Suzanne," my therapist said in a comforting voice. "You are likely suffering from adrenal fatigue. Adrenal fatigue can cause people to experience depression or thoughts of self-harm." A light in the corner provided enough illumination to see while creating enough cover for me to admit my perceived frailty. "The good news is this thought scared you. If it had soothed you, provided comfort in any way, I would have you admitted to the hospital. But I must ask, what can you do to reduce your stress levels? What can you remove from your life so you feel like yourself again?"

"Nothing," I said as I played with a tassel on the couch pillow. I couldn't fuck it up. I was ashamed to tell people I was struggling, to admit I couldn't handle it. Because admitting to that would constitute "fucking it up."

I am lucky, I know. I got help. I pulled myself together. A few months later I was admitted to the partnership. And for several years, I loved my job. The pressure I put on myself throughout the partnership admission process lifted. I had fun. I learned new things and was challenged. The work was fast-paced, and I had lots of carrots in front of me. I was respected for my title and my accomplishments. I had arrived. From the outside, it seemed like I had it all.

On the inside, it was a different story. You can only run from yourself and the systems you have created for so long. Soon enough the pace and expectations caught up with me. The stress returned. I was exhausted again.

Is this all there is? The voice was a whisper in the back of my mind—gentle and quiet, like aspen leaves rustling in the breeze.

Because I thought I had it all, or at least everything I had wanted and worked for, I pushed the thought down. I ignored my intuition by focusing more on work. I juggled my commitments—work, home, and personal, spreading parts of me around so I could say I was giving attention to everyone in my life. Most of the time I prioritized work. When I had time left over, I'd elevate the priority of my family, friends, and my well-being. Unintentionally, I made the people who should have been my priorities optional. Ultimately, I discovered everyone, especially me, was dissatisfied with this system.

I needed something different. I needed time and space to slow down, to figure out what I was supposed to be doing. I needed more than a vacation. *But what?* Stepping away for even two weeks always seemed like a lot in the moment. *How could I step away for longer? I would lose everything I had worked for.*

People at the top of their game just don't walk away. But then again, what would happen if I stayed? What would it cost me in the long run? My relationships, my family, my happiness, my health? Living every day just to get through it is no life.

Both sides of the equation scared me, so for a long time, I did nothing.

* * *

If you are or someone you know is struggling, experiencing suicidal thoughts, or in crisis, help is available. In the United States you can call, text, or chat 988 to be connected with trained mental health professionals with the 988 Suicide and Crisis Lifeline, formerly known as the National Suicide Prevention Lifeline. These trained counselors will listen, provide support, and connect you to additional resources, if necessary.

CHAPTER THREE

THE MAIL

Courage is one step ahead of fear.
—COLEMAN YOUNG

"We can't go," I said, my voice small.

"What? Why?" Bill said, turning to look at me. He stood several feet ahead of me on the hiking trail.

"The mail," I replied, reaching up to remove my sunglasses so I could see Bill better in the shadow of the tree cover.

"The mail?" he questioned, adjusting his baseball cap.

It was mid-morning, and the trail to Looking Glass Rock in North Carolina was filled with people ascending a steep switchback. A haze of humidity hung in the air as the late July heat overtook the brief relief provided by an earlier rainstorm. Bill and I left our rented cabin early in an attempt to reach the summit before the afternoon thunderstorms would move in like clockwork. And while all of this was going on I had managed to bring the foot traffic to a virtual standstill because of the mail. People tried to pass us while keeping the required social distance of the pandemic and trying not to slip down the muddy embankment to a lower switchback.

"Yes, we can't move to Mexico. What will we do about the mail?" I asked. My anxiety was rising.

Deciding to move to Oaxaca was easy. Executing our move was proving a bit more difficult, partially because I had no idea how to execute a move like this and partially because our decision to move was so quick.

I started with a list of big things I intuitively knew needed to get done. Arrange for a sabbatical with work, make sure passports and visas were in order, find a place to live, and tell our kids, family, and friends. These tasks all seemed doable and logical, something that could be tackled with a well-developed project plan. But five days after making our decision, while out on a hike, the thought of the mail popped into my head, and it suddenly seemed like an insurmountable challenge.

Bill scrutinized me. His face showed bewilderment, a bit of amusement, and a hint of exasperation, but his voice was patient. "We can't move to Mexico, because of the United States Postal Service?"

"Yes, the United States Postal Service," I said seriously. *What is he missing about the gravity of this situation?*

"What is the problem with the mail?" Bill asked gently. By now he had walked back to where I stood. We had shimmied our way up the hillside and out of the direct flow of the hiking traffic.

"Well, how will we get it? Can we stop it? What if it builds up and that's how people figure out our house is empty and they rob us?" I rambled on. It was clear the train to "Crazy-town" had arrived at the station. *Suzanne Roske, party of one—all aboard!*

Bill smiled, turned, and began walking again, "I am not talking about the mail. We will figure it out, but I am not focusing on the mail."

I was stunned and somewhat offended. Fear bubbled up within me—fear of making an impulsive and potentially life-changing decision to move to Mexico without understanding and planning for all the ramifications.

How many times had I approached other decisions by looking at the pros and cons of the alternatives in front of me? I would become almost paralyzed by the decision that stood before me. On more than one occasion, I grabbed onto one pro or con of a potential decision like a life raft that allowed me to stay within my comfort zone. I regretted many of those decisions when I had opted for safety instead of taking a risk.

As Bill continued up the mountain with our dog, I realized I could either look for and find every small objection that would allow me to remain right where I was, in my comfort zone yet unhappy, or I could choose to not let the mail stop me. I could take the risk, have a fallback plan, and jump into the adventure. *Who knows what will happen?* On that mountainside, I chose not to let the mail stop me. Whenever things started to feel big or scary—and that happened a lot—I would remind myself I wasn't going to focus on the mail. I was opting for adventure; I was betting on myself. The mail wasn't going to stop me.

CHAPTER FOUR

EXPLANATIONS

We all make choices, but in the end, our choices make us.
—KEN LEVINE

"We have news. We are moving to Oaxaca, Mexico," I said to the blank stares of my children.

We had dropped the kids off at summer camp exactly thirteen days before we made this announcement. Before Arlington County Public Schools announced school would be remote in the fall. Before we had any thoughts of moving to Mexico. A lot can change in two weeks. We sat in a park across the street from the Chick-fil-A, explaining our plans to move to Oaxaca over chicken sandwiches and lemonade. Emily, Zane, and Quinn looked at us in a state of mild disbelief.

"You're joking," Emily said, pulling a long sip of her lemonade before chomping on her nugget ice.

"Nope, not joking," Bill said. The kids looked from one another and back to us. They didn't protest or throw a fit, but rather showed confusion and wanted an explanation.

"School will be remote in the fall, and we just can't see them switching to in-person school before spring. Once it gets cold, it'll be really hard to be inside all the time," I added. "The weather is great in Mexico, so we'll be able to get outside."

"Mom and I have always wanted to live internationally, and this seems like a great opportunity. It will be an adventure," Bill continued. The kids' faces didn't budge, not a smile or even a nod. I moved into what I thought was the hard-press sales mode.

"Look, we found a house with a giant pool," I said, handing Zane the phone so he could look at the pictures of the house we had arranged to rent. "And there is an aviary. With peacocks. Did you see the peacocks?" The phone passed from Zane to Quinn to Emily. The kids weren't tipping their hands if they thought any of this was impressive.

Bill saw my "hard-press" for Oaxaca wasn't getting us anywhere, so he jumped in. "You guys can do things in Oaxaca you've wanted to do in the US but haven't been able to. Quinn, you can ride horses. Zane, look at the mountains; there must be some really good biking there. And Emily, Oaxaca is filled with artists; you can take painting and pottery classes." Bill appealed a bit more to their desires. It seemed like maybe he was making some headway in convincing them this move could be a good thing.

Quinn, who hadn't touched her food, was picking blades of grass from between her legs when she looked up and quietly asked, "What about Tilly?"

With authority in my voice that didn't match any knowledge in my head, I said, "Baby, Tilly is our dog; she is family. She comes with us. I promise." Tilly, our anxiety-ridden dog, hated riding in the car. How on earth would she handle a plane ride? I honestly had no clue how we would get her to Oaxaca. I looked at Tilly. *Please fit under the seat on the plane.*

TELLING FRIENDS

"You're moving to Mexico? That's brilliant! What did the kids say?" My friend Molly and I were on a walking date as I explained our plans for the first time. It was a conversation I would need to put on repeat over the next few months.

"They seem good with the idea. Bill and I are a little surprised, to be honest. I wouldn't say they're excited, but they aren't fighting it either." I would learn later Emily was pissed about our decision to move to Mexico. At thirteen, moving away from your friends, even if you can't see them in person, was hard. Emily accepted our decision was made, so she said there was no use fighting it.

"It's because they trust you," Molly said confidently. "This trip will be great for them. What an adventure! Have you told your boss? What did they say at the firm?" Molly was upbeat about the possibilities before us. Her enthusiasm was contagious.

But not everyone was so supportive. "This just seems like an unnecessary risk for you and your family. I mean for one it is Mexico. There is so much crime. And what about the pandemic? If you get sick, you are stuck. And what about work, Suzanne? This seems like picking up the hammer and nailing yourself inside your own coffin," said another friend. I was surprised as this friend had always been a big international traveler, so to hear their concern caught me off guard. Thoughts like these were enough to make me question our decision from time to time, as I didn't want people to think we were being irresponsible.

TELLING WORK

"I need a break to figure out what I am going to do next. My family needs me. COVID is taking a toll," I said to one person after the other at my firm. To my amazement almost everyone was supportive. One person told me I was making a potentially career-ending mistake by taking a sabbatical (picking up that hammer and those nails again) and another felt we were going to be kidnapped and held for ransom. But by and large, my colleagues' support was positive.

"This is amazing. Having to supervise work and school is just too much. What a great idea!" other working parents said.

"I am so tired, but I honestly have no idea what I could do beyond the firm. It is my life," confided some of my partners.

"We are going to highlight your plans on an upcoming webcast. It will be great for you to share your experience with our flexibility policies," said our internal team.

"You are so brave. This is a courageous decision," many said to me. I felt anything but.

TELLING MY PARENTS
"Are you sitting down?" I asked, sitting in my bedroom/office and looking directly into the video camera, trying to project some amount of calm and confidence. It was a month and a half before we were set to leave. One-half of each of my parents' faces was visible on the computer screen; they were still working out the kinks of video calls. I had been scared to tell my parents we were moving. I wasn't sure they would understand. They would miss us. Even when you can't see each other because of quarantine, something about being in another country makes the distance feel greater. I shouldn't have worried.

"Suzanne, you and Bill need to do what you think is best for your family," my dad said. "These kids are suffering from the restrictions of COVID. And you haven't seemed happy in a while. Your mom and I think this is a great idea. We will come to Arlington to say goodbye before you leave." Whether they really thought our decision was "great" was beside the point. Having the support of my parents meant the world to me.

But ten days before our flight was set to leave, my dad called to tell me he wasn't going to come say goodbye to us after all. He didn't want to put their twelve-year-old dog in a kennel for the weekend. He would stay home with the dog. I was too stunned to ask questions or to argue. Later, while taking a shower, I replayed the conversation. I was overcome with the thought I might never see him again.

What if he got sick? What if he died?

My throat tightened, and my breath was stuck. I leaned against the side of the shower, slid to the floor, and began to sob. My fears were unleashed as water poured over my head.

Was I being selfish by making this move?

My internal shitty committee chimed in with their opinions.

Of course you're being selfish. You are taking their grandchildren to Mexico. And for what? So you can find yourself? Who said you were entitled to be happy?

And let's talk about selfishness. The reason he's not coming to say goodbye is he wants to bring his dog with him, and he knows you don't like dog hair in your house. What's up with that? Of course you have a designer dog that doesn't shed. You are shallow. Just let the man bring the dog.

And in case you are wondering, yes, you will regret this decision if either of your parents gets sick while you are off galivanting in another country.

My shitty committee can be loud and mean.

I sat on the shower floor with my emotions until I began to wrinkle from the water. When I was ready, I stepped from the shower and grabbed my phone. "Dad, it's me. I don't like dog hair, but I love you. And we have a vacuum cleaner. Please come; bring the dog."

When you announce to friends and family you are leaving for eight months, you never know what to expect. People I thought would question our choices were fully supportive, while some of the more adventurous folks in our circle questioned our judgment. At some point, I realized I didn't need anyone's approval to make this move; I certainly appreciated it and welcomed their support, but I was moving to Oaxaca for me.

CHAPTER FIVE

FAMILIES STAY TOGETHER

> *Family is not an important thing. It's everything.*
> —MICHAEL J. FOX

"Families stay together!" Quinn shouted at the top of her lungs.

The heads of fellow passengers turned to look at us. The normal buzz of Ronald Reagan Washington National Airport was reduced to a whisper. My family was becoming a spectacle.

The five of us were scattered in front of the American Airlines ticketing agents. Seven duffle bags were perched across two luggage carts and were leaning precariously like the Tower of Pisa. Our carry-ons, including a bass guitar, a sewing machine, and a ukulele, were strewn around our feet. Tilly, our seventeen-pound, long-legged mini-labradoodle refused to lay down in her carry-on crate. Tilly proved to be the first challenge in getting to Oaxaca. The agents said she was too big to go on the plane.

It was October 3, 2020. I was as ready as I could be to depart for Oaxaca. I had done everything I could think of to prepare my family. We had our Mexican visas. The house was buttoned up, and friends were watching it so it looked like someone was home. The mail was being held by the US Postal Service. Amazingly, they have a way to handle the mail I was so panicked about. We started Spanish lessons with a teacher in Oaxaca. For me this was critical as my Spanish at this point consisted of the few phrases that got me through a week's vacation in Cancun; think "please," "thank you," "where's the bathroom?," "can I have a beer?" That wasn't going to cut it living in Mexico.

I even bought a dog carrier in early August so I could get Tilly comfortable in it. A few times throughout the day, I would stick Tilly in the carrier, and she would fall asleep. I practiced walking her around the neighborhood, so she'd be used to it moving. Admittedly, I felt like a fool walking the streets with my dog in a bag in the oppressive August heat and humidity in Northern Virginia. But the one thing I knew was a bit of a crapshoot in this whole move-to-Oaxaca plan was the dog.

You see, the airline's guidelines for traveling with a dog in the cabin were a bit vague. She had to be fewer than twenty-two pounds (or twenty-five by some accounts), fit comfortably in the carrier, and not touch the sides while laying down. *Check, check, and check.* Ultimately, however, the decision to allow a dog onto the plane was at the discretion of the ticketing agent. Tilly had long legs—so long when the agent went to check Tilly in and asked for us to take her out of the carrying crate, she popped out like a jack-in-the-box.

"That dog can't fly. It's too big." The agent's tone held a finality to it. She offered us a few alternatives.

"Your first option is to leave the dog at home," she said. *Okay, not really an option as we're moving to Oaxaca.*

"Your second option is to check the dog. It would fly under the plane like luggage," the agent said. "Unfortunately, because of COVID, we aren't checking animals at this time." *Also, not really an option, is it?*

"Or you could get the dog certified as an emotional support animal," she said.

"Great. What does that entail, and how fast can it happen?" I asked, grabbing for the paperwork in the agent's outstretched hand.

Now, I am good at logistics. I can rally teams, my family, hell, strangers in situations that require working together, pointing us all toward a common goal. I can coordinate the timing of planes, trains, and automobiles to get us to our destination on time. But I am terrible when my emotions are highly charged and the situation calls for calm, rational thought without any immediate action.

Bill, on the other hand, can stay calm, cool, and collected in situations like this. So I turned to Bill and gave him the look that said, *I am not the one who should be handling this.*

While Bill proceeded to calmly talk through options with the ticketing agent, I sprang into action. Action masks anxiety; this was my wheelhouse.

Could I get Tilly qualified as an emotional support dog? At the moment, surely, I needed some emotional support. I called my friend Rosie, who is like a sister to me and happened to be a registered nurse. "Would you sign the airline's form stating I need an emotional support animal?" I blurted into the phone, without so much as a hello.

"Um, okay," she said. "But are you sure you don't need something stronger?" Rosie's ability to break through my nonsense with a single sentence made me realize just how manic I must have sounded. She signed the form anyway. With the emailed note saying I needed an emotional support animal in hand, the next step was getting a signature from our veterinarian. Our vet wasn't open, so I contemplated if I could forge their signature. *Nope, I couldn't do that.*

I reluctantly retreated to the ticketing area and our piles of bags, joining Quinn and Zane. Bill was still patiently speaking with the ticketing agents. Emily was next to him, calming Tilly. I was at a loss as to what we should do next.

Quinn looked at me with wild eyes, big and blue, tears on her cheeks and a fair bit of snot on her nose. "What are you going to do?" Quinn asked. "You promised Tilly would come with us."

And there it was. This was my plan. My big idea. *You made promises you can't keep.* I felt the weight of my promises and my decision closing in on me. Suddenly the move to Oaxaca felt like something I was doing to them. *You are selfish and self-indulgent. We haven't even made it out of DC, and your plan is already falling apart.*

"Worst case, you, Emily, Zane, and Dad will fly to Oaxaca today. I'll stay here and figure out what we do with Tilly and meet you there in a few days." I said, once again trying to project an air I had it all under control.

Quinn stared at me with an indignant expression. She was shocked by my suggestion. She exploded, "Families stay together!" She was right. Of course, she was right.

"Oh, baby!" I said as I pulled her into my arms. Zane pulled us both into his. With the eyes of the ticketing hall upon us, we had a Roske hug—a Quinn sandwich with her smushed between Zane and me. We stood there for a minute or maybe three, until Quinn started to wiggle.

"It's hot. I can't breathe," she said, which is always how a Quinn sandwich ends.

Something happened at the ticketing desk in the moments we were hugging. Another agent came out. They talked and gestured a lot. Bill and Emily smiled. Tilly was laying down in her crate. Bill looked over, gave us a thumbs up, and waved for us to bring the luggage.

He had done it! Bill's calm had prevailed! I am not 100 percent certain what Bill said that convinced them to let Tilly on the plane. Something about us moving to Oaxaca and Tilly not being a puppy (somehow, they thought she was five months old, not five years old). Whatever it was, we were through.

Something else shifted in those moments—okay, it was closer to an hour. If you happened to have been stuck behind us at Ronald Reagan Washington National Airport on that October morning, I sincerely apologize for your delay and our antics. But in those moments, we came together for a common purpose. Zane calmed me down. Emily calmed Tilly. Bill exercised his strengths in helping others see alternative ways of looking at a situation. And Quinn came up with the most important lesson: families stay together. It was not about our things, what we were leaving, or where we were going. It was the five of us, or six with Tilly, were doing this together. We were doing this as a family, and that was all that mattered. In those moments, Oaxaca was no longer my dream or even Bill's and my dream. It had become our dream—the Roskes' dream. We were about to walk onto the plane to make it happen.

CHAPTER SIX

ARRIVAL

You must trust and believe in people or life becomes impossible.
—ANTON CHEKHOV

"Is this a truly insane idea?" I asked. We had called our friend Tom, who was living and working in Mexico City, to get his perspective on our idea to move to Mexico. Tom is equal parts optimist, pragmatist, and lover of international experiences, so we were eager for his input.

"No, it's not insane," said Tom. "I think it is brilliant." I was relieved. Now for cities to consider. "I would recommend Merida or Oaxaca," said Tom. "Both are wonderful cities and are also large enough for access to health care should you need it."

"What about the beach?" I asked. "A surf town like Sayulita or Puerto Escondido." Images of bare feet, aqua-blue water, surfing, and palm trees ran through my mind.

"I wouldn't recommend the beach," said Tom. "The Wi-Fi is notoriously unreliable. You'll likely see a lot of expats, so you won't need to speak Spanish all that much. Plus, Bill doesn't love the beach. He'll be bored within three weeks."

Tom struck down my "what about the beach" suggestion with reasonable points. *Damn him.* We had been to Merida before. Lovely city, a bit large and humid. So I Googled Oaxaca. One look at the search results, and I knew it was where we were headed.

As we told our family, friends, co-workers, and neighbors of our plans to move to Oaxaca, they had many questions. Where would we live? What about school? Were we going to work? What about COVID? But the most frequent questions surrounded safety.

"Isn't Mexico extremely dangerous?" "What about the drug cartels?" "Aren't you worried about getting kidnapped?" "Will you live in a gated community, with a security guard?" The perception of Mexico as a universally dangerous place was prevalent among almost everyone we spoke with. Well, perhaps not dangerous enough to deter vacations to the all-inclusive resorts in the Riviera Maya, Cabo San Lucas, or Puerto Vallarta, but dangerous, nonetheless.

As a general rule, I believe most people are good and aren't out to get us. I applied the same thought process when thinking about Oaxaca. We'd take normal precautions. We'd try not to do anything to put ourselves in a compromising or dangerous situation. Above all, I would trust but verify. This is how we operated in the US, and we'd follow the same plan in Mexico. But the US is different from Mexico, which probably seems obvious. My plan to trust but verify was always not possible. I had limited information to verify or people to verify with. I simply had to put my faith in others.

"Hold on," said a friend incredulously. We were standing on the balcony of a country club celebrating a colleague's retirement, but much talk had turned to my sabbatical and move to Oaxaca. "You only have a verbal agreement to rent a house in Mexico. There's no contract?"

"Nope. No contract," I said with a bit of hesitation. Saying out loud we were moving to Mexico without a formal agreement to rent a house sounded a bit silly. I gathered my resolve. "I've seen pictures of the house on the internet, so it exists. And I've talked to the landlord. He's a young guy, Abdias Escobar. He seems nice."

"Escobar? Like Pablo Escobar? The drug lord?" he questioned, eyebrows raised, an air of *holy hell* in his voice.

I laughed in a dismissing manner, "Escobar is a common last name."

"This is not good, Suzanne. You are being naive. It's a setup. You're going to get down there and they're going to rob you, extort you, or kill you." He had real concern in his warnings.

"Don't be ridiculous," I said. "It's going to be fine." But a seed of doubt had been planted in my brain. *Would it be fine? Yes, it would be fine. It had to be fine.*

Fortunately, our arrival in Oaxaca was much more uneventful than what our friends had warned us about. We emerged from the airport into the warm evening air and were greeted by a driver with a "¡*Bienvenido* Roske!" sign. Relief washed over me. Abdias, true to his word, had arranged for a van to meet us at the airport and take us to our house. We made it!

As we drove away from the airport, I expected to see colonial Spanish buildings and large laurel trees. Everything I knew about Oaxaca I had learned from the cultivated pictures of Google. Unfortunately, our first views of Oaxaca didn't live up to these expectations. It was dark. Like, no streetlights, no light pollution. The streets were marked with potholes and aggressive speed bumps called *topes* that appeared at close but random intervals. The buildings were industrial or in a state of construction. I saw a lot of exposed rebar.

"Look there's a KFC, a Walmart, and a McDonalds!" the kids said, as they talked over one another. *Fabulous—we've arrived in Oaxaca's version of America.* This was not what I had been dreaming about.

As we got farther away from the airport, the buildings changed from industrial big box stores and fast-food restaurants to the colonial and Spanish styles I had envisioned. The light allowed us to take in our surroundings.

Massive laurel trees, adorned with twinkle lights lined the side of the road. People slowly walked along the sidewalks, out for what I assumed was an after-dinner stroll. *This was more like it.*

We began climbing a gradual hill, leaving Centro and the city behind us. We headed toward the mountain foothills. The lights disappeared, and it was dark again. Eventually, we turned from the main road into what appeared to be an alleyway. Somehow it was darker. The walls were covered with graffiti. Dogs barked in the darkness. We started bouncing in the back of the van as the road became even rougher. It felt ominous.

This is it. My friend was right. It's a scam. It's going to end right here in this alley. I'm about to die, and I haven't even had a real Mexican taco. They are going to steal our money and our stuff. Please God, spare the children. And the dog! Spare the dog. After all, it took to get her here, please spare the dog!

As my thoughts spiraled to images of the terrible outcome about to befall us, we made another turn and the alley opened onto a road dotted with gates to homes. Up a hill, around a corner, and at the end of the cobblestone road standing beneath a purple jacaranda tree were our landlords. They stood in the street welcoming us into the home that would be ours for the next eight months. Abdias, dressed in a cool leather jacket and high-top sneakers, looked like he just arrived from Mexico City. His father, Señor Abdias, had a rumpled yet friendly look to him. And Abdias' mother, whose name I never learned but whom we called Señora Abdias, wore a long red skirt, high heels that brought her height to barely five feet, and a stern expression. They took us in as we spilled out of the van—the kids, the dog, our stuff. We were a sight.

"*Hola*. Welcome! How was your trip?" asked Abdias. "You must be hungry. We have food waiting for you. Let me help you with your bags." I exhaled; it had been a long trip. The kids scattered into the house to pick out their bedrooms, with Tilly chasing after them. Abdias and Señor Abdias reached for our bags. Señora Abdias smiled and gently guided me into the house. I took a mental picture of the scene before me: the Abdiases' welcoming us, the kids running into the garden to look at the pool, and the dog jumping and barking at her newfound freedom. It felt like home.

I chuckled as I compared this welcoming scene to the scene of death I had just created for myself. I had overreacted certainly, but my inner dialogue revealed I, too, had been influenced by the stories I'd heard in the US. The dangers of Mexico are replayed by the media and had been reiterated by friends and family. I had made a snap judgment. How could I have honestly believed these good, kind people who would eventually become like family to us would want to harm us without even knowing us?

It was not who I was, nor the person I wanted to be. I resolved then and there to trust people were generally good. If I wanted to live with integrity and make a life here, I needed to trust and treat the people we met the way I wanted to be treated. Not fearful. Not suspicious. Not judgmental. Not creating barriers that didn't need to be there. It is a way we should all strive to live. But this would prove to be a necessary resolution because little did I know at that point just how much blind trust I would need to put into the people I met in Mexico.

CHAPTER SEVEN

TEAM COLORADO

Friendship is born at that moment when one person says to another, "What? You too? I thought I was the only one!"
—C.S. LEWIS

"You did what?" asked Bill, poking his head into the kitchen.

"I invited the family from Colorado over to swim," I said, as I organized the peanuts and veggies for our guests. Bill looked at me with a quizzical look. "You know, the family we met last week at the market in Centro. The one with the monk."

"The family with the monk?" Bill asked, obviously confused by my explanation, which seemed clear to me.

"No," I said laughing. "There was a Tibetan monk at the market. The family had two kids. A boy and a girl. About the same ages as Emily, Zane, and Quinn. They're moving from Colorado to somewhere in Central or South America. I didn't catch that part."

"You mean the people we talked to for like two minutes, while Zane was in the bathroom? The lady who said the guanabana juice was good? Those people?" Bill asked, catching up with the order of events that had transpired a few days ago.

"Yeah, that family. I found the woman, LeAnn, on the Oaxaca Expat Facebook page. I sent her a message and invited them over this afternoon."

"We don't even know them. What if they're crazy? What if we don't like them?" Bill asked as he grabbed his biking gear and headed to the patio to ready his bike for a quick ride in the hills near our house.

"Let's face it; we're all here in Mexico. So we're all somewhere on the crazy scale. The question is how far to the left or right," I called out to Bill from the kitchen. "Besides, they'll only be here for a few hours. The kids will swim and play. If we have nothing in common, they'll leave, and we'll be no worse off. How bad could it be?"

I understood Bill's confusion. I'm an introvert. I can work the room and take center stage when I need to, but I prefer to be at home with my family and my people. It was out of character for me to stalk a family on the internet, find them, and invite them over (well, the inviting them over was out of character; the Facebook stalking, not so much).

Connecting with strangers was way more in Bill's wheelhouse than in mine. In fact, he had been the one to strike up the conversation with them in the first place. But I knew if I wanted to make friends and find my people in Oaxaca, I was going to have to put myself out there. Inviting Team Colorado—our collective nickname for the whole family—over that afternoon was one of my first attempts at putting my commitment into practice.

Team Colorado arrived at our house with chips, guacamole, and *cervezas* in hand—a promising start. The kids stood on opposite sides of the pool, reluctantly dipping their toes into the water. They weren't swimming or talking to one another. The familiar pull from their toddlerhood, when kids' playdates needed to be orchestrated, tugged at my heartstrings. Would I insert myself today, offering conversation starters like "Do you guys like Minecraft? Because Zane and Quinn *love* Minecraft." or "Do either of you like running? Because that is Emily's thing." If I inserted myself, I would inevitably end up on the receiving end of a my-mom-is-so-lame teenage eye roll. Because let's face it, it would have been lame. So I kept my mouth shut, hoping they would find a way to break through the awkwardness on their own.

"We're moving to Costa Rica to open a bed and breakfast," said Marty, as he grabbed a beer and stuffed a lime into the can.

Costa Rica—that was it!

Team Colorado left Denver earlier in the summer. They crossed into Mexico in Tijuana, their Chevy Tahoe filled to the brim with household goods, four people, and two giant Swiss Mountain dogs. "The border patrol agents barely gave us a second glance," continued LeAnn. "We traveled south through Baja California, stopping for about a month in La Paz, just north of Cabo San Lucas. We stayed there for about a month hoping to get in some beach time."

"But the beaches were closed due to COVID, so we crossed from Baja over to the mainland on a ferry, which was more like a cargo ship," said Marty. LeAnn and Marty had a smooth back-and-forth rhythm to the story, which allowed each of them to grab more chips as their story unfolded. "The dogs weren't allowed on deck, so we were basically stuck in our truck for fourteen hours."

Splash, splash, giggle. The kids were in the pool. My anxiousness receded a bit.

"So we're taking our time, but admittedly getting a bit anxious to get there. The border to Guatemala is closed for at least a month, so we've rented a house and are exploring and eating our way through Oaxaca."

"Why did you pick Costa Rica?" I asked, although I had a zillion assumptions as to why: the beach, the mountains, the rain forest, the surfing, the sunsets, the sloths, and so on.

"Actually, it was the kids' idea. We were on vacation in Costa Rica in 2018. One night at dinner the kids said, 'We should move here.' It was an interesting idea that quickly took hold. We explained living in Costa Rica wouldn't be like a perpetual vacation. They weren't too happy they'd actually need to go to school," explained Marty.

"Initially, we thought we'd move down for a year, but we got to thinking, *Why not longer?* As a family, we decided we'd commit to having both kids finish high school in Costa Rica, so we're in for the long haul," LeAnn said, also more relaxed now the kids were laughing and having fun.

I was in awe.

I thought we'd taken a leap with an eight-month move to Oaxaca, but Team Colorado was fundamentally restructuring their lives. They'd sold their house and most of their things. They bought a property they were going to renovate and open a bed and breakfast, even though they'd never run a B&B before. They were driving almost five thousand miles across Central America, which honestly was the craziest part for me. And their commitment was for at least nine years until their kids were done with high school.

In comparison, our decision to shutter our home in northern Virginia (it would be there if we needed to pull the plug on this adventure), have our kids Zoom into their school day in Arlington, and live for less than a year seemed positively pedestrian. Before hearing their story, I felt a little bit daring. Now I felt like a bit of a sell-out.

"We want the kids—well, all of us really—to experience more of the world. We want to immerse ourselves in the community and the schools, so moving to Costa Rica made sense to us," explained LeAnn. I understood. That is what we wanted too, albeit in a much shorter timeframe.

"If we can get there," said Marty nervously pulling at his T-shirt, "as we don't know how long the border to Guatemala will be closed given the pandemic." Team Colorado had been on this adventure for a few months and were eager to get settled in their new home.

"We'll get there, even if we have to fly. We'll just get the dogs qualified as emotional support animals," said LeAnn reassuringly. I groaned thinking about all the trouble we'd had with Tilly.

"It's wonderful we've all changed the trajectory of our family's lives, for good or bad. We're all on an adventure. Cheers." She raised her glass as a toast to our collective adventure.

"Cheers," the four of us responded in unison.

Team Colorado were our first friends in Oaxaca. They softened our landing into our new yet temporary life. Their children provided companionship for mine. They were peers to share a laugh with and people to look at and know they weren't alone in their family's plan to try something different—whether for the short or long term. LeAnn became my hiking buddy, and Marty served as our entertainer, *asado* (grill) starter, and tech support. But more than that, Team Colorado was an inspiration of what could be.

They showed us how to take calculated risks so we could embrace the culture more fully. Do you want to eat street food? Do it; just look for the stand with the longest line of people. Do you want to go to the *Central de Abestos* market, the big market where tourists generally didn't go without a guide? Do it; just leave your wallet and phone at home and go get the decorations for the Day of the Dead altar. You're worried about drinking the water? Have a beer instead.

They showed us what it meant to be flexible. When the world threw speed bumps at them, they adjusted and moved on. After a month and a half in Oaxaca, when the border to Guatemala still wasn't open, they got their giant dogs qualified as emotional support animals and shipped their truck so they could get started on the rest of their life.

They confirmed it takes courage to make a bold decision to change your entire life, to leave the safety and comfort of what you know. It doesn't matter how far you go or how long you go for. Personal growth comes when you change the trajectory of your life and open yourself up fully to new experiences—because on the other side of risk, and sometimes the daily struggles of living in a developing country, are happiness and fulfillment, acceptance of yourself, and connection with your family.

Most importantly, they reinforced life as I had known it in northern Virginia didn't have to be the same. In Team Colorado, I saw myself. Others were feeling restless and looking for something different, even though the path they were taking to realize what they were supposed to be doing was different from mine. They showed us we weren't alone. They are our friends, and for that, I am forever grateful.

CHAPTER EIGHT
GOLDEN THREADS

> *There is no greater gift you can give or receive than to honor your calling. It's why you were born. And how you become truly alive.*
> —OPRAH WINFREY

"*Maíz*, or corn, is the golden thread that ties all *Oaxacaqueños* together. *Maíz* originated in Mexico over ten thousand years ago. It runs through our communities, connecting us across all time. *Maíz* feeds our livestock and our souls. It runs through who we are and what we do," said Betsy Morales with deep reverence in her voice.

We were on a food tour, and Betsy, our guide, was explaining the important role corn has played in Oaxaca's way of life and traditional foods throughout history. Corn is essential in Oaxaca, and it is everywhere. Corn grows in fields across the countryside and in the smallest gardens in the city. It grows straight up the mountains and dots the deep valleys between the hills. Corn is the foundation of almost every dish in Oaxacan cuisine—from tortillas to tamales to *tejate*, an ancient drink made with corn and cacao.

"Have you ever had a taco or a tamale without corn?" asked Betsy. "Of course you haven't!" She was holding court as we sat at a picnic table in a market. She was proud of her heritage and pleased to share a taste of what made Oaxaca special—at least from a food perspective.

"What about soft tacos on flour tortillas?" asked Emily as she reached across the table to grab a *limonada*.

"Oh, those? Well, they aren't real tacos," Betsy said with a smile and a wink. As if to prove her point, Betsy waved her hand above the smorgasbord of food set on the table before us. In all the dishes, corn was the primary ingredient.

As a lover of food, I was in gastronomic heaven. I popped a *garnacha* into my mouth, which resembled a bagel bite, Mexican style. Aside from burning my mouth, the *garnacha's* similarities to a bagel bite stopped there. The base of a *garnacha* is a thick corn tortilla fried to a golden brown. It is topped with sweet chili salsa, shredded pork, crumbled queso, and cool sour cabbage. The ingredients mixed and performed a happy dance across my taste buds.

"Yum. This is good," Quinn said through a mouthful of food. She pulled a *memela* away from her mouth. The melted Oaxacan cheese formed a thin connection to the toasted tortilla covered with pork lard, refried beans, and cheese. *Memelas* are simple, warm, and filling. It is no wonder why they are served as breakfast, lunch, and dinner staples in Oaxaca.

"And now for the *tlayuda*. It's like a Mexican pizza, but much better. *Tlayudas* are what Oaxaca street food is known for," said Betsy. "Did you see the Netflix special about street food? Oaxaca's *tlayudas* were named the best street food in the world." She placed the oversized blue corn tostada, covered with pork lard, beans, cheese, lettuce, grasshoppers, and pico de gallo onto the table.

Three hours remained on this food tour. *I should have worn stretchy pants.*

Betsy's reference to a golden thread—an idea or feature present in all parts of something that holds it together and gives it value (Oxford Learner's Dictionary 2022)—had me wondering, *If maíz represented Oaxaca's golden thread, what was mine?*

I have two core values: making a difference and authenticity. It was easy to recite them. I mean, I narrowed it down to two so I could remember them. But what did these values mean to me? Was I honoring my values in the work I did, the decisions I made, and how I lived my life? I wasn't sure I had the answer. But if I wanted to figure out what I was supposed to be doing, I had to figure out how I was, or more likely wasn't, living my values.

Merriam-Webster defines authentic as being "true to one's own personality, spirit, or character" (Merriam-Webster 2021). For me, it also means bringing the best of myself and my strengths to every situation. The truth was, however, my leadership style was a mashup of the styles of the successful leaders I had worked with. More often than not, these leaders were older, white men.

This isn't surprising given I spent most of my career working within the aerospace and defense (A&D) industry. A&D has come a long way in terms of gender diversity, but in the late 1990s and early 2000s, it was dominated by men. As a young professional, I was often the only woman in the room.

I quietly observed the leadership styles of the men in my work life, working hard to adopt their behaviors as my own. Don't get me wrong; many men I worked with had great leadership qualities. But overall, success seemed to rely upon jovial jokes, pats on the back, taking up space to stake your spot, and knowing it all. It wasn't really me, but as the adage goes, "Fake it, until you make it."

No matter how hard I tried though, *faking it* never felt right. So I experimented with ways that would allow me to integrate "work" and "home Suzanne" as a whole person. I started by sharing my stories.

"Being successful in this job can be challenging," I said to a ballroom packed with newly promoted managers. They wanted to understand what it was like as you moved up the ranks within the firm. They were eager and already looking for their next carrot. "You will make a lot of sacrifices. Traveling every week can be difficult. You need to know when and how to set boundaries. There was a time when both my husband and I were traveling for work. I returned late one night and headed straight to the babysitter's to pick up my toddlers. I was tired and stretched too thin. On the drive to our house, I fell asleep at the wheel. I woke up just before I ran straight into the jersey wall."

"What did you do?" a female manager asked from one of the tables halfway back in the cavernous ballroom. In the dim light, I could barely see her face.

"Well, I told my husband I couldn't do it anymore," I said, shifting on the stage. The lights suddenly felt hot. "After much debate and discussion, we decided he would take another job where he wouldn't have to travel so much." Someone in the audience groaned. The men I could see were rolling their eyes. The few women in the front of the ballroom looked dismayed.

My goal was to let the new managers know I also had a life beyond my career. I understood the trade-offs the job required and how exhausting it could sometimes be. I struggled with balance. Instead, I'd highlighted my privilege; my spouse was able and willing to shift his career focus so my career could flourish. I'd attempted to be vulnerable, to share a moment that had scared me and made me question my priorities. Instead, my story felt forced. I hadn't made a big move. I'd just adjusted my circumstances so I could continue to prioritize work. I didn't feel authentic. I felt exposed and weak.

As I pulled at my golden threads unraveling the leader I was, I didn't like what I saw. I didn't like the way I was living my life. I wasn't being authentic to myself and to what I believed in. I wasn't making a difference in the way I wanted to. I tried to introduce more of who I was into my work persona, approaching problems with an air of exploration and creativity. I had the desire to experiment and take risks with new subject areas. Sometimes the new approach was appreciated, but more often than not, I was met with skepticism.

So I retreated to comfortable and safe projects, back into the lane everyone expected me to operate in. I pushed down thoughts about doing something different and stuffed the skills that made me unique into a box because I had experienced the downsides of trying to bring all of me to the office: not feeling heard, valued, or seen. My lane might have seemed boring, but it was safe. I didn't take on big risks, which left less room for error. Soon, I became apathetic at work and frustrated at home. I took my frustration out on those I love most.

"Bill. Guess what? I am not a miserable person!" I said skipping into his Oaxacan office, triumphant with my discovery. I spoke loudly to be heard over the washing machine that was working beside his desk. I held out a piece of paper with a classic management consulting two-by-two matrix scribbled on it for him to see.

He glanced from the paper to me. "I don't think you're a miserable person," he said cautiously because I had sort of come out of left field with this statement. He couldn't tell where I was going to take this.

"Hear me out," I said. "I'm not being authentic and I'm not making a difference—at least not the way I want to be. I performed an energy audit of my day-to-day activities. And guess what?"

"An energy audit?" Bill asked, raising an eyebrow and the inflection of his voice.

"Yes, an energy audit," I said, realizing until this point an energy audit was something we had done to our home in Virginia to see if cold air was leaking through the windows. I needed to provide a bit more context. "I looked at all my day-to-day activities, what I do at work and at home. I looked to see if these activities drained me of energy or recharged me. Sort of like a battery." I handed the matrix I had drawn to Bill. It was covered with the titles of the jobs and roles I assumed over the years. Each job had been assigned an emoji—happy, sad, and meh faces—representing how I felt about each of these roles.

Leaning over Bill's shoulder, I explained the two-by-two: "See, I'm happier when I am working with people. Directly impacting them. Being a mom, teaching classes, facilitating experiences, working in a hardware store, developing innovative and creative ways of working. And over here," I said pointing to the other square, "I'm less engaged when I am doing work that impacts the broader institution, which is how I spend most of my day. The activities I spend most of my time on drain me. I'm not recharging my battery. And when I get home, I have nothing left to give to you and the kids. So you see, I'm not miserable. I am just burnt out. Isn't that great?"

Bill was skeptical. I was relieved. For a long time, I assumed I was a miserable person who was taking my misery out on my family—the ones dearest to me. But I wasn't miserable. I was just in a lot of situations that caused me to feel miserable. I was depleted and burnt out. I couldn't be of service and express my love in an authentic way. That was different from being a miserable person. I was in control. I could change my situation and the path in front of me.

If I wanted to show up differently at home, I needed to show up differently across all aspects of my life. Embracing my strengths and celebrating what I love to do. Serving people. Being creative and facilitating experiences that allow people to see possibilities in themselves they hadn't seen before. Cultivating connections between people and ideas. Leading from behind, supporting the people I work with. Helping them listen to their hearts so they can follow the path they were meant for and be the best of themselves. This is what I wanted to do more of. This is how I wanted to show up at home and work. I didn't know *what* I was going to do at this point, but at least I knew *why* I was going to do whatever I did. I had discovered my purpose.

The golden threads that run through our lives are our most important values. They influence the decisions we make and the impact we have on others. Unfortunately, in a world where we are moving fast and trying to keep up, it is easy to lose sight of what is important. I certainly lost the connection with my golden threads. It wasn't until I took a hard look at how I was living my life I saw, like the corn in Oaxaca, my golden threads were all around and within me. I could choose to ignore these threads, or I could embrace and honor what makes me unique, what I am called to do. I will intentionally sew together the tapestry of my life in a way that will let my golden threads shine.

CHAPTER NINE

SILENCE

Listen to the silence. It has much to say.
—RUMI

I was raised on a tiny strip of land off the coast of New Jersey. Seven miles long and a quarter mile wide. The Atlantic Ocean was to the east; the Inter-coastal Waterway was my backyard. Saltwater and sand run through my veins. I believe salt water will cure almost anything. Got a cut, stick it in the bay; hungover, jump in the ocean; thirsty...nope, that's one of the few things saltwater won't fix. I love the expansiveness of the ocean. I can get lost in the waves, but I find myself there too. When I need to center myself, I head to the beach and the ocean.

It was a picture of the Pacific Ocean that caught my attention. An advertisement for a women's meditative yoga retreat in Mazunte, Mexico. The ocean seduced my senses. The idea of a meditative yoga retreat made me nervous. I suck at both activities. Meditation results in my ever-present, intrusive thoughts creeping in or I fall asleep—that's it, no middle ground. As for yoga, I've always been more of a fan of tortuous endeavors, like running marathons, suffering through boot camps, or other forms of exercise where people scream at you. But I'd committed to trying new things. So I said yes to the beach and a meditative yoga retreat.

The thought of driving across the mountains to the beach was daunting. It was only 240 kilometers, or 150 miles, from Oaxaca de Juarez to Mazunte, but it was an almost seven-hour drive due to the curving roads. *What if I break down? What if I get lost? How will I communicate with anyone?* Between the distance and my broken Spanish, I decided it would be best to find a co-passenger for the trip.

"You just found a girl to go with you?" Bill asked. He was working and half listening to me as I rambled on about the upcoming retreat, the car I'd rented, and the stranger I'd arranged to be my co-pilot. The last part got his attention.

"Yeah, she's also going to the retreat," I said. "Don't worry, I stalked her on Facebook. Her name's Tess. Seems normal. It'll be fine." Tess hailed from the Bay Area and had lived in Mexico for three years, so her Spanish was solid. I'd pick her up at the airport on the way out of town. It was all arranged. *Why's he so concerned? Does he honestly think she's a serial killer or something?*

"You look just like your Facebook pictures," said Tess. *Ahh, so you stalked me too. We're gonna get along just fine.* "I need to call my boyfriend; he's afraid you are a serial killer or something. You can talk to him. Let him know you won't kill me," Tess said, laughing as she reached for her phone and threw her backpack into the rental car. *They thought I was a serial killer. Interesting.*

"So tell me your story. Why are you in Oaxaca?" asked Tess as we pulled away from the Oaxaca airport. She was chatty; I was relieved by my decision to offer Tess a ride. Within thirty minutes, we'd left the city of Oaxaca de Juarez behind and were climbing toward the expanse of mountains ahead. The road started to curve.

"So I get car sick," said Tess. "I don't throw up or anything, but I do get groggy. I'm going to climb into the back and go to sleep. Wake me when we get to the beach." Tess awkwardly climbed between the front seats, settled herself in the back, and donned a sleeping eye mask. There went my company and began my weekend of silence.

The scenery changed quickly from the dry, high-desert plateaus of Ocotlán de Morelos to the tree-covered foothills of the Sierra Sur. We reached San Jose del Pacifico, a quirky little pueblo nestled in a valley of mountains at eight thousand feet elevation. Everyone says it is the halfway point to the beach; it's not. We still had a long way to go.

The main street of San Jose del Pacifico was crowded gringos. A twenty-something crossed in front of me, his hair dreadlocked, wearing cargo shorts and no shoes. Behind him was a group who looked like they had just walked out of The North Face store, clad in khakis, puffer jackets, and backpacks. They were ready for a hike. Traffic slowed to a crawl as tourists weaved between small *tiendas* and wooden mushroom carvings of all sizes. San Jose del Pacifico is known for its beautiful mountain views and for the abundance of hallucinogenic mushrooms that grow wild there (I did not stop for the mushrooms). Town lasted for about two hundred yards. Once again, the road curved and undulated ahead of me before disappearing into the clouds.

Tess continued to sleep.

Logging trucks barreled around tight corners taking up both lanes. Minibuses sped by, making their round-the-clock runs between the beach and Oaxaca. A few cyclists biked on the road. They were a different breed. The engine of my little Toyota screamed as we pushed uphill; how badly were their leg muscles burning? I couldn't let my focus wander, since the road had no shoulder. Now and then, I had to relax my grip on the steering wheel to let the blood flow back into my fingers.

Soaring pine trees surrounded the road. Occasionally, a break in the trees would open to a vista. A quick sideways glance rewarded me with views of the mountain expanse that seemed to go on forever. I drove above the clouds. As I crossed the mountain pass at the peak elevation of the drive, I was thankful for the opportunity to witness the changing landscape. The clouds soon parted, and we descended into banana fields. The humidity rose as we approached the Pacific.

Tess slept on.

The paved road turned to dirt but continued onward. More mountains were in front of me. Even though Tess was snug in the back seat of the car, I was alone with my thoughts. I was glad for the distraction of the road because I was not one to sit with my thoughts for long. I actioned through them. And then, just as the silence became more than I could bear, the Pacific Ocean came into view. Once again, the ocean had saved me from me.

I wasn't saved from the silence or my thoughts for long. Day one of our meditative retreat was a day of silence. "If you can't sit with your thoughts, then who will sit with you?" our retreat leader asked.

What the hell? She sounds like one of those motivational posters. This was not in the itinerary. Ahh, the judgmental side of my internal shitty committee had arrived.

But you said you were going to try new things. The encouraging side retorted in a sarcastic tone. But it was right. I had come too far, so my thoughts and a journal were mine for the next twenty-four hours.

Oh my god, was it hard! My thoughts wandered everywhere. *I should call Bill and the kids. It's hot. Why is one little mosquito so loud? Should I walk to the ocean? What are the other people thinking about? When's dinner? What do you call a guy digging a hole? Doug—ha! Our father who art in heaven.... How does the rest of it go?*

Stop it! Do something. Do anything.

I tried drawing. Writing. Watching the waves of the ocean roll in and out. I walked. I napped. I felt itchy and thought the only way to scratch the itch was to talk. It was a weird feeling for me as I am usually pretty reserved and quiet, but somehow when I wasn't supposed to talk, all I wanted to do was to say something—anything—out loud.

I would love to say I eventually found peace in the silence, but honestly, the silence just wore me down. I got tired of fighting my instinct to fill the silence with thoughts or activities.

I just sat. I just was.

Space and quiet opened in my head. I wish I knew how it happened, mostly so I could find my way back there again. At some point, I grabbed my journal and began writing not about me, not about my feelings, not about the tangible things I wanted. I wrote about what I wanted my family to think of me. The things I wanted Bill and the kids to know. Things I wanted them to truly understand about my love for them if I were not around tomorrow. I wrote what they likely thought about me today. A gap existed between my ideal state and my current state. I needed to close the gap.

Eventually, I wrestled with my thoughts around my career and what I wanted to do when I returned to Virginia. The pressure I had felt for years. I was unhappy, and it wasn't just a COVID thing. I acknowledged those feelings. I cried—not sobbing tears, but more of a cathartic release of the stress I'd been holding in. I was utterly lost and had no idea what I wanted to do despite my best efforts to figure it out. It felt elusive.

I'm not religious, but I consider myself spiritual. I believe we are on this earth for a reason. I believe we can unlock our full potential. I believe a higher power is out there; maybe it's God or maybe just the universe. Either one can guide us if we ask and listen.

Please help me figure out what I'm supposed to be doing.

The sun was setting. I wandered to the balcony overlooking the ocean. I sat in a hammock, and the sun dipped toward the horizon. My thoughts were quiet and settled when my inner voice broke through.

Design. I want to design.

This thought startled me. I am not a designer. But the voice was loud, clear, and directive.

I want to design.

I tried to push the thought aside. I didn't want to go back to school to become an interior designer or graphic designer. What was this? I wasn't sure, but I intuitively knew the voice had spoken. Honestly, it freaked me out a bit.

I slowed down and quieted myself enough to hear my internal voice that provided me with direction. Now I had a job to figure out what it meant because it wasn't a whim, but the direction from the universe, my inner sage, or the depths of my soul. I also knew it was just a piece of the puzzle, not the entire picture. I still had a lot of work to do.

CHAPTER TEN

MAGGOTS

> *We can do hard things.*
> —GLENNON DOYLE

"Maggots! We've got maggots!!" I screamed from the kitchen. The terracotta floor was covered in tiny, white, wiggling maggots.

One thousand one. One thousand two. One thousand three. Aside from the pounding of my heart, the house was silent. No one was coming to my rescue. Granted, it was a Wednesday morning. People were working and in school, but still, I was in the midst of a crisis. Where was everyone?

"We have maggots!" I shouted again, louder this time. Finally, I heard doors opening and footsteps moving throughout the house.

"What's going on?" Bill asked as he crossed the courtyard from his office to the main house.

"You okay?" Zane asked as he poked his head through the open window from the balcony into the kitchen.

"What's up?" Emily and Quinn asked as they appeared at the door to the breakfast room.

They arrived at the same time looking only mildly concerned about being summoned by my shrieks. "We have maggots!" I repeated with a slight shrill in my voice.

"What are maggots?" asked Quinn. Zane volunteered a quick overview that maggots are fly larvae shaped like rice. "Ew, gross!" Quinn said turning on her heels and retreating quickly from the scene.

"That sucks. Gotta get back to class," said Emily with an air of *what do you want me to do about this?* in her voice.

"Sorry, Mom," said Zane, as he reached through the window grabbing a banana before disappearing from my view.

Bill surveyed the scene. I stood stone-still like a statue, no shoes on, maggots everywhere. "What would you like me to do? Get the broom and dustpan?" His voice was calm, unfazed, and emotionally detached from the gravity of my situation.

A dustpan and broom? Are you kidding me? How can you be so calm? This is absurd! Don't you know me? I'm the woman who threatened to sell our house and move because of an ant infestation. And that was just ants, for God's sake. I'll admit my reaction to ants was dramatic. I can handle almost any other type of bug: cockroaches—I'll squish them; spiders—I'll rescue them; things with lots of legs—I'll praise them for eating mosquitos. But ants make me feel dirty. As I stood, blankly staring back at Bill, I discovered maggots freaked me out even more than ants did.

They're crawling up my legs. They're so itchy. Get them off.

"Stop jumping around, Suzanne," Bill said. "You are scattering the maggots. You're just making it worse."

"I can't. They're on me; they're gonna suck my blood and eat my flesh. Like in the movie. *Stand By Me.* When the maggots attacked Corey Haim and River Phoenix."

"Those were leeches, not maggots," Bill said with a laugh. "Maggots won't suck your blood. They probably came from the trash." He turned walking to the service area to get the supplies to clean up the mess.

The trash can. That makes sense. The empty trash can sat across the room. Just before I discovered the maggot infestation, the bell for the trash truck had rung, indicating it was at the end of the street. I'd gathered the garbage bag, which included the remains of a whole chicken from the market yesterday, grabbed a few pesos to tip the garbage man, and hustled down the street. When I returned, I found myself standing in a sea of maggots.

Bill was back at the kitchen entrance. He poked his head in the door and placed the broom and dustpan inside the threshold. *I notice you didn't enter the kitchen but stayed far away from me and my little friends.* Somehow the mere fact Bill was keeping his distance was enough to make me feel slightly better about the situation.

"Here you go. You may want to mop and clean out the trash can with bleach, too," Bill said as he returned to his office.

Thanks, Captain Obvious. I grabbed the broom and got to work cleaning up the maggots.

Maggots became symbolic. I don't like them, but I can handle them (because, yes, I had the pleasure of dealing with maggots on several more occasions. Lucky me!). I learned, though. I adapted. I tied up the chicken carcasses in plastic bags to keep the maggots at bay. I used a bit more bleach. If I can handle maggots, what else could I handle? Pushing through the unknown to see the possibilities of a life that could be—sure. Wrestling with the discomfort and risk of switching to a new career path after twenty-five years—definitely. Doing something that made me happy instead of what was expected of me—that sounded great.

Although the kids still make fun of me and imitate my initial shrieks of "we've got maggots," my reaction evolved to quietly cursing under my breath rather than summoning the entire house. Maggots happen, and I can handle them. I can do many things when I don't want to but know I have to. And although I acknowledge maggots won't suck your blood, I do insist on showering immediately after cleaning up... with maggots, you can never be too sure.

CHAPTER ELEVEN
PIÑATAS

You can be rich in spirit, kindness, love, and all those things that you can't put a dollar sign on.
—DOLLY PARTON

I love Christmas.

I love the traditions and the time with my family.

I love cooking recipes that have been passed down through generations. The kinds that require you to watch your great-aunt Marie mix the pot pie dough because she doesn't have a written recipe and insists half a teaspoon of salt goes in the dough (it's one *tablespoon*, by the way).

I love shopping for the perfect gift that will make someone smile.

And I love heading to the local tree farm to find the fattest Christmas tree possible. Bill and the kids think I am nuts, but they go with me every year and begrudgingly stand near potential fat trees, while I run around looking to see if it is *the one*. Oaxaca doesn't have any Christmas tree farms, so what is a girl to do? Find the biggest, fattest Christmas *piñata* possible, that's what.

In late November, colorful Christmas *piñatas* started to appear in doorways and at the roadside *tiendas—piñatas* of all shapes, many sizes, and lots of characters. But I hadn't seen one yet that fit my "biggest, fattest" requirement.

"*Quiero compar una piñata de Navidad.* (I want to buy a Christmas piñata)," I said to the woman who cleaned our home.

Esmeralda came to our house two times a week. I tried to make small talk with her. She generally avoided me. I assumed it was because my Spanish was so terrible. As usual, Esmeralda went about her cleaning, saying nothing in response to my *piñata* statement. So I was shocked later that day when I received a text from Esmeralda; her cousin makes *piñatas*, and she would have him make one for me.

And so it was on a Tuesday evening in early December when Quinn, Emily, and I went to the other side of the city to pick up our *piñatas*. As we drove, the wind picked up and a chill settled upon us as the sun began dipping toward the mountains in the west. Finally, it felt like cooler weather was coming.

I turned off the main road, onto a potted dirt road. We bounced through the potholes and over the *topes*. Stray dogs ran beside us barking as our truck kicked up a cloud of dust behind us. Ahead of us, the road ended in a cornfield, and to the right was a small *tienda*, where *piñatas* swung in the wind. A corrugated tin fence ran from the *tienda* around the corner. A man wearing a plaid shirt, faded blue jeans, and a cowboy hat stepped into the road. He directed me around the corner, where we found Esmeralda's extended family waiting.

Señor Carlos greeted us and waved us through the gate. We were followed by what seemed like a dozen kids, three dogs, and several cats. Inside the gate, chickens pecked at the ground and several women stood by a steaming pot hanging over an open fire. This was not their yard; we had been invited into their home.

The floor was dirt and most of the area was open to the sky; dust whipped around us in tiny dirt devils driven by the wind. A long table that sat under the corrugated metal roof and a small cinder block structure housed the bedroom. The women noticed us, three blond *gringas* standing in their home, they smiled warmly. A flurry of activity followed. An older woman with graying hair braided into long plaits handed me a glass of *agua de piña* (pineapple water) and a bowl of pumpkin seeds. Emily and Quinn had been offered the same. We graciously accepted and expressed our thanks as Carlos, his wife, mother, and sons ushered us into the *tienda* to show us the *piñatas*.

Their *piñatas* were magnificent. The ones Carlos made for us were at least five feet in diameter and covered in multi-colored mylar paper. They also had small and medium-sized *piñatas*, as well as *piñatas* shaped like trees, snowmen, Santa, elves, and brightly colored Christmas bobbles. The family talked over one another, excitedly pointing from one *piñata* to another. Pride radiated from each family member. I wanted all the *piñatas*, the two large ones we had ordered, and the smaller ones. "Mom, that's enough," Quinn said under her breath after I picked out five additional *piñatas* to decorate our home with.

Carlos' family was thankful for our purchases. He helped us tie the *piñatas* into the back of our truck and offered to teach us how to make a *piñata* after the holiday season was over. We waved goodbye to the large, loving family, as we set off into the darkness for home. It was strangely quiet in the car compared to the large family's cacophony of sounds.

Emily broke our silence. "They were so welcoming, so proud of their work, and so excited to share it with us," she said. I shifted my eyes from the road momentarily to glance at my daughter. She had a quietness about her that seemed to foreshadow a deep thought. "They had almost nothing but gave us something to eat and drink. They barely had a roof over their head, but they were happy." Emily paused again, collecting her thoughts and her words. "I could tell. They had each other. Everything they needed." I let out a breath I didn't realize I had been holding. Emily made a profound observation, but I had felt it too.

Carlos' family was happy. For all the time I had spent chasing success and relishing in the admiration of others, I realized I wasn't as happy as this family was. Before leaving for Mexico if you had looked at me, you would have seen a person who arguably had it all, who was objectively successful yet was empty. The praise, money, and stuff only made me want more. And I was afraid if I slowed down, I would lose it all.

On the other hand, I just witnessed a family who seemed to have nothing, yet somehow had everything. They had one another. They had the work that made them proud. They had music playing on the radio and hot soup cooking on the fire. What more did they need? I knew at that moment the secret to happiness was not more, but less. I went to Carlos' for the biggest, fattest *piñatas*; what I received was perspective. And what a gift that was.

CHAPTER TWELVE

THE GODDESS WITHIN

When you stop living your life based on what others think of you, real life begins. At that moment, you will finally see the door of self-acceptance opened.
—SHANNON L. ALDER

"A goddess lives deep inside each of us. She is in your heart, your belly, and your womb, which is known as Yoni in Sanskrit. Throughout this weekend you will connect with the goddess of your Yoni. You will let go of your self-doubt and you will embrace self-love," JoJo announced in a voice that was melodic and hinted at her Australian heritage. My fellow *goddesses* and I were seated in a circle on a rooftop overlooking the ocean. The sun was setting. The smell of incense and burning sage circled my head. They mixed with the salt air and hung a bit heavier in the humidity. Eyes closed, I held hands with a woman whom I had met earlier that day. When I registered JoJo's words, my eyes popped open and I stared at her.

Oh, hell no!

Even though I don't practice anymore, I was raised Catholic, where guilt is a way of life and self-love should probably be added to the list of cardinal sins. Some lessons run deep and tapping into self-love was going to be hard. Despite my discomfort, I breathed deeply because I was here to push myself into new territory, and apparently "nurturing the goddess within me" was part of the deal. *Focus. Quiet your inner chatter. Concentrate on your breathing.* It was going to take a miracle for me to find my inner goddess.

JoJo continued speaking to the group with her eyes closed. I took advantage of the opportunity to study JoJo in a way that can only be done when you break the rules and open your eyes. JoJo projected confidence and calmness. She was in control, in her element. She commanded the space with authority I'd rarely seen, even in boardrooms. Her feet were bare and her hair tussled. JoJo wore a flowing linen dress; it was clear she wasn't wearing a bra. She seemed so comfortable with herself, in her skin, and in this space.

While JoJo and the other women seated around her radiated beauty, I felt awkward and insecure. Not feelings that support finding your inner goddess. My thoughts drift quickly to my position, my title, and my income. These objective measures of success should have brought me a level of confidence similar to JoJo's. They didn't. Instead, I was ashamed I equated success with my position and bank account. I was also sad. I wasn't sure I could ever match the level of authenticity JoJo possessed.

I stared, transfixed on JoJo's bare feet and my thoughts drifted to my relationship with footwear, specifically high heels. I have always viewed high heels as my "super suit"—my version of a superhero's cape. When I needed to feel confident, I would don a pair of heels. I am fairly tall, so when I wear heels I can usually approximate the height of the men in the room. I can look them in the eye (or close enough). The men can't look down on me, at least not in the literal sense. Whatever the situation, I felt I could hold my own when I wore heels. Even packing for Mexico brought the decision of whether to bring a pair or not.

"Why are you packing high heels?" Bill asked as I tried to shove eight months of clothes and shoes into a duffle bag. It was late September. We were in our bedroom packing, trying to determine what we would need for eight months, without much idea of what that was.

"Well, what if we meet people and go to a party? I need heels," I responded.

"You *need* heels?" Bill asked. His view of needs generally followed Maslow's hierarchy where food trumped all else.

"Yes, I need them. I feel more confident in heels. They're like my superpower," I said as I zipped up the duffle with a force that signaled the conversation was over.

As a side note, I tried to wear the heels one time while in Mexico merely to prove I hadn't brought them in vain. Within seconds of stepping out of the house, I rolled my ankle on the cobblestones and landed on my hands and knees in the street. *So much for giving me superpowers.* I immediately switched out of the heels and put my Birkenstocks back on.

As my thoughts returned to the rooftop, I vaguely heard JoJo announce our evening activity: dancing. Dancing by ourselves. Dancing with a partner. Dancing while standing in a circle as the other women danced around us, supporting us as we embraced the goddess within. There was probably more, but I didn't hear it.

The thought of dancing made me uncomfortable. I felt vulnerable and exposed. I generally don't dance. I mean I'll dance in the kitchen with my family, but in public, nope. No dancing unless copious amounts of alcohol are involved. I retreated to stand by the balcony railing, swaying imperceptibly. I felt physically incapable of doing anything else. It was taking all my effort to stay where I was. All I wanted to do was to run away and get some space. *If only I had my heels; I'd have confidence. I would dance.*

But would I have danced? Would my heels have made any difference? Probably not. My discomfort could not be masked by an article of clothing or footwear. I was afraid of what people would think of me if they saw me dancing. This was the barrier I needed to break through. To stop worrying about the judgment of others who I couldn't catch the beat or my dance moves would look spastic. To find a different way of being. One that acknowledged and embraced who I was and who I wanted to be. Because I didn't just hold myself back when it came to dancing. It was across all areas of my life. I was afraid of being judged, afraid of looking silly. On the other hand, looking silly seemed like a far better outcome than putting on heels and potentially breaking an ankle.

"Now, I invite everyone to close their eyes so you can *hear* the message of the next song." JoJo's melodic voice interrupted my inner monologue. Darkness had settled around us, making it hard to see anyone. The breeze shifted and brought in cooler air from the ocean. As the music started, I closed my eyes, let go of the railing, and slowly moved to the center of the palapa.

The melody was rhythmic. The artist's voice was deep and guttural. I was jolted by the messages within the song:

Being authentic. Being who you are. Not trying to fit into a mold. Knowing you are unique. Knowing your value. Knowing you are enough.

The messages of the song spoke directly to me. I surrendered, eyes closed moving to the rhythm of the music, overcome by emotion. Without meaning to, I danced. And I shed a few tears—tears because I didn't believe I was enough. I was always striving to impress people and worrying about their judgment. I put on heels to give myself superpowers, but I was pretending. Tears because although I liked what I had accomplished, I didn't like or even know all of me. Tears because I knew if I wanted to change my life if I wanted to be more authentic and allow others to be more authentic, I needed to accept me for me. Accept all of me. The good and the bad. My strengths and insecurities. As I danced, I felt a strange warmth inside of me, maybe it was my inner goddess or maybe it was just the heat and humidity. But whatever it was, I was opening up to the possibility I too could be free. I just needed to take off my heels.

CHAPTER THIRTEEN

FAMILY VALUES

Creating a family identity is the collective equivalent of imagining your best possible self.
—BRUCE FEILER

What is the meaning or purpose of your life? I sat staring at my computer screen, the blank Google doc taunting me because I didn't have an answer to this seemingly simple yet ridiculously loaded question. I started crafting draft statements, paused, reread, and immediately deleted them. Again, and again, and again. I was stumped. A few years ago, we created a family mission statement. That had been so easy, so fun. I remembered with vivid clarity the night three summers before when we worked as a family. I let my mind wander to that night.

You get a lot of strange looks when you walk into an office building on the Friday evening of Labor Day weekend, loaded down with craft supplies, magazines, and three young kids. It was 2017, Emily and Zane were both ten, and Quinn was six. Bill's office in Washington, DC, was eerily quiet as everyone, except for a few custodians, had cleared out earlier that afternoon heading to the beach, the pool, or a barbecue for summer's last hurrah.

Yet here I was, begrudgingly following my family into a conference room to create a family mission and values statement. I was not happy, I wanted to be one of the people at that pool. Unbeknownst to me then, the events of that evening would become one of my favorite things we'd ever done as a family.

When I was pregnant with my twins, I read almost every book I could get my hands on that explained how to raise happy, healthy children. *What to Expect When You're Expecting?* Check. *The Happiest Baby on the Block.* Check, check. *How to Talk So Kids Will Listen and Listen So Kids Will Talk.* Check, check, check. However, once my twins were born, I abandoned the luxury of reading anything beyond *Goodnight Moon*, threw out all the preconceived notions I held about raising these tiny humans, and strapped in for the wild ride that is parenthood.

Fast-forward ten years, and by all objective measures, my family was doing great. No cavities for the kiddos. I could usually get them to write thank you notes for gifts they receive. They were doing well in school. Bill and I even manage a date night now and then. Not too shabby.

So I was surprised when Bill came into the living room where the kids and I were playing a rousing game of Monopoly, and said, "I just read this book called *The Secrets of Happy Families*. It was great. I want you to read it. I think it'll help us."

Someone told me once it typically takes six seconds for a brain to respond to a stimulus. I have no idea if this is factually accurate, but if it is, I am an outlier—an overachiever, shall we say—because I react immediately. And in response to Bill's request, my face immediately revealed my confusion. *But we* are *a happy family,* and displeasure, *oh God, not a book report.* Bill quickly cut off the objections I was preparing.

"I picked out two chapters, just two, I think are most important," Bill said. "I'm only asking you to read two chapters. Please." Bill rarely asks for much, and this was "just two" chapters of a book, so I figured I could do that. My silent protest, if you can call it that, was I wouldn't read the book, but rather I'd listen to the audiobook. Oh, the rebel I am!

As a surprise to no one but me (I mean the book was a *New York Times* bestseller), I found some interesting nuggets connecting leading business practices to successful family dynamics. The book offered up interesting perspectives. Things I hadn't thought of before made a lot of sense. I could see how many business practices should be applied to a family system from budgeting to goal setting. But the one that stuck out to me was also the one Bill was interested in: creating a family mission and values statement. This made perfect sense. I could see the benefits.

This brings me to Labor Day weekend and the corner conference room, overlooking the National Mall and the Washington Monument. We covered the conference table with sticky notes, old magazines, poster board, scissors, glue sticks, and markers. The whiteboards were clean and ready for our ideas. We played music to liven the mood. We had ourselves the makings of a dream design thinking session.

Bill facilitated. We created vision boards of what was important to each of us now and what we wanted our family to be in the future. We drew pictures and covered the windows with sticky notes that captured our values. We took turns presenting our ideas and listened to what each of us had to say. We danced a bit. A few mic-drop moments occurred, especially when Zane announced, "We work hard because dinner ain't gonna pay for itself." We laughed endlessly—deep, knowing laughs that come with the familiarity of family and the strength of love. As the sun slowly sank behind the Washington Monument, a picture of my family emerged—kind, adventurous, willing to be uncomfortable, imaginative, silly, creative, loving, introspective, opinionated, smart, tenacious, daring, and compassionate.

Beyond creating a family mission and values statement that night, we cemented a memory I will treasure always of the five of us simply being together, designing the path we want to walk and deciding how we would hold one another accountable for how we show up. The five of us created our mission and values statements.

The Roskes: We Are Kind, Smart, and Tough

- Experiences are better than stuff
- We are active outsiders
- We are curious, lifelong learners
- The greatest wealth is health
- We build others up with our actions and words
- We work hard because dinner won't pay for itself
- Attitude is the difference between an adventure and an ordeal
- We are flexible, we take risks, we learn from our mistakes
- We are like muscles: we may get sore, but we won't stop
- Family is where life begins and love never ends
- We do it with humor

We took pictures of our mission and values statements before we left for the night. We were proud of our hard work. I had every intention of having an artist capture the words in a painting to hang in the house. That never happened. We had every intention of incorporating our family values into our everyday lives, but we didn't. Not really. From time to time, one of us would quote one of our values, but that was where it stopped. Our family values were more of an afterthought rather than the guiding force we'd set out to create.

Sitting at my makeshift desk, I pulled out the pictures of our family mission statement and re-read the words we had collectively developed. I realized this statement, crafted with the ones I love most, is the meaning of my life. It is the best version of our family and me: to be active, to learn, to try new things, to help others, and above all to laugh.

CHAPTER FOURTEEN

FAILURE

I have not failed ten thousand times; I've successfully found ten thousand ways that will not work.
—THOMAS A. EDISON

"This looks like a piece of shit," I muttered under my breath.

"Yup," said Emily, smiling. She was in her element throwing clay in the pottery studio.

I was working on what was supposed to be a coiled clay pot. Instead, it looked like a pile of dog excrement that could be found dotting the streets of Oaxaca thanks to the large population of stray dogs. We were standing in the back room of an art studio. My fellow classmates were hunched over a low-slung wooden table, sweat dripping from their brows. A door was cracked to let in some amount of fresh air. But the tiny stir of a breeze was no match for the tin roof that trapped the midday heat, turning the pottery studio into our own personal kiln.

Emily was making a little bowl she was deftly molding into the shape of a cow...cute. Two young women from Germany sat across from us, chatting with an Aussie about their recent trip to the beach town of Puerto Escondido. They were sculpting a plate and accompanying mugs. At the end of the table, an older gentleman was also working on a coil pot. But his piece looked remarkably like a pot. Everyone but me appeared to be mastering this little clump of mud.

I was failing! Mission accomplished! My reaction might seem a bit odd, but I was taking this pottery class for two reasons. First, Emily had asked if I would take the class with her, so of course, I was there. And second, this week's assignment for my leadership class was to do something you've never tried before and you are sure to fail at initially.

Failure. I know I am supposed to see the value in it. I have read articles containing pithy little slogans like "failure is life's great teacher" (Estrem 2021). Intellectually, I understand if you succeed in everything you do, you are likely not pushing yourself far enough. But honestly, I don't like to fail. Never have. *Merriam-Webster* defines failure as 1) omission of occurrence or performance; 2) lack of success; 3) falling short; and 4) one that has failed (Merriam-Webster 2021). Nothing about any of these definitions sounds fun. It is no wonder why I have tried to avoid failure almost my entire life.

I've always been a striver, an overachiever, and a perfectionist. I'd work on client deliverables long past the point of enhancing the value. My goal was to avoid negative feedback, to impress, and to only receive praise. I held my tongue in meetings if I felt my ideas weren't perfectly crafted. I wouldn't try something new for fear I wouldn't be good at it right off the bat.

Perfectionism seemed to be the price of admission to do well. How many times had I heard from eager candidates in job interviews their biggest flaw was being a perfectionist? It was drilled into us that providing this response would turn a negative (your biggest flaw) into a positive (perfectionism). But what was the cost of striving to be perfect both personally and professionally? Ideas not explored, risks not taken, and learning opportunities missed.

I wasn't thrilled with an assignment where I had to purposely fail, but I figured I could rig the system with pottery. *You're artistic. Pottery will be easy-peasy-lemon-squeezy. You'll try it, succeed, and submit this assignment about how you didn't fail because you are just that good.* I know that sounds conceited. And boy, was I wrong. To prove how wrong I was, here is how my afternoon trying to make a small, clay coil pot went:

"Your first step will be to take a large piece of clay from the bag. You want to gently massage the clay by combining a kneading action with a rocking motion. Look here," said our instructor, Patricio, showing us what he was describing.

I grabbed a large hunk of clay from the table. Almost immediately I was engaged in a battle royale with the clay. It stuck to my hands. It stuck to the table. The clay was in my hair and all over my clothes. Nothing gentle or rhythmic was going on. "Gently, Suzanne. Strength is not required," said Patricio upon seeing my struggle. My clay resembled something out of the sci-fi movie *The Blob*. It was not the smooth, supple orb Patricio had created. My clay and I had started out on the wrong foot.

"Now you will form your clay into a cylinder," said Patricio as he moved on to step number two. Patricio placed both of his hands in the center of the cylinder, rocking them back and forth from the center of the clay to the ends. He quickly transformed his cylinder into a two-foot-long rope of clay.

I tried to follow along with Patricio and formed a squatty, little cylinder. Looking back, that should have been the highlight of my day. From that point forward, my hands refused to move evenly. I couldn't "rock" the clay without causing an earthquake-like shake for the rest of the table. My fellow artisans glared at me. I gave them a sheepish smile. The clay began to tear into small six-inch sections. And then I found an air bubble—apparently, the point of the first step was to remove the air bubbles, so back to step one I went.

I repeated steps one and two. By this point, Patricio was gracefully coiling his two-foot cylinder of clay upon itself to make a pot. He gently smoothed the clay, clapped his hands, and stood back in admiration of his pot.

My clay rope was uneven and brittle. The clay wouldn't coil. It snapped into pieces as I tried to build the pot. I kept going, wrapping the broken pieces on top of one another. *Maybe it'll look better from a different angle.* I turned my head awkwardly to look at my creation. Unfortunately, that wasn't the case. "This looks like a piece of shit," I said exhaling in frustration.

"Yup, it sure does look like a pile of shit," said Emily, a little too loudly and too enthusiastically for me.

Our classmates looked over in response to Emily's comment. They started laughing. I had to appreciate the absurdity of the situation. A hunk of mud had gotten the best of me. I laughed. Our collective laughs echoed against the tin roof.

I supposed I should have been more comfortable with failure because life in Oaxaca was a daily experiment in failure. Honestly, it wasn't a matter of if I would fail, but more a matter of how many times and how big the failure would be. I didn't consciously stop to think about all the times I had failed, though. I simply adjusted, course-corrected, laughed at myself, and moved on. In these failures, there was no judgment, or if there was, I didn't care. I'd simply found a way to not get something done.

Not caring about what other people think was an attitude that had eluded me my entire life. I had always felt the risk had been too great, the weight of the judgment of others too heavy. But in Oaxaca, I was free to take risks and experiment. I had to. I needed to get stuff done. I wasn't ashamed because I was trying and learning. And I found I liked living in this constant state of relearning and adjusting.

I eventually overcame my coil pot failure. I asked for help and got some pointers from Patricio. My failed coil pot transformed into a smooth-edged, passable shallow bowl. All it took was a little water, some fresh clay, perseverance, humility, and a bit of humor. Not only did I come to appreciate failure that day, but I also found a major appreciation for all the lopsided clay pinch pots my kids had made for me every year for Mother's Day.

CHAPTER FIFTEEN

ESMERALDA

The shoe that fits one person pinches another; there is no recipe for living that suits all cases.
—CARL JUNG

It's hard to put yourself in someone else's shoes. We try our best to have compassion; try to be empathetic and understand the facts and circumstances behind situations; try to be objective and caring. But the truth is sometimes the shoes are too tight, worn in the wrong places, or just don't fit us. Esmeralda's shoes were this for me.

I only knew a few concrete things about Esmeralda. I knew she cleaned our house and her cousin made *piñatas*. Most everything else I gathered through observation. Esmeralda was a petite woman in her early thirties, with large, soulful, brown eyes. She wore a serious expression and a chain around her neck with a butterfly on it. Esmeralda was punctual, arriving every Tuesday and Thursday by 9:30 a.m. Her commute was almost two hours each way. She took three buses from the other side of the city and walked the final three-quarters of a mile from the bus stop to our home. From the moment she arrived to when she departed in the afternoon, Esmeralda flitted; that is the best word I can use to describe her. She was in a constant state of movement, half walking, half running. She didn't stop moving and she never sat down. Esmeralda seemed to embody the butterfly charm she wore.

Esmeralda was distantly related to our landlords, so she was to be trusted. She was paid the equivalent of twenty US dollars for six to seven hours of work. For a service professional in Oaxaca, this was a good job and a good wage. It was a bit shocking for us to see the Mexican class system unfold before our eyes. Though trusted to clean our house, Esmeralda was not supposed to use a bathroom inside. Rather, she was supposed to use the bathroom in the separate service quarters, but we used this room as Bill's office so the whole thing was a bit weird. As I came to understand the *rules*, the domestic help was not supposed to take breaks, get water to drink from the house, or eat lunch. I had a real problem with this. It took me well over a month to convince Esmeralda I seriously wanted her to take a break, refill her water bottle, and eat lunch with food I provided if she wanted to.

Esmeralda didn't speak a word of English and generally avoided speaking to me at all. When she needed to communicate with me, she opted for a rare text message or hand gestures. Her go-to gesture was to circle her pointer fingers around each other, again and again, with me trying to guess what she meant. Over the course of our time together I figured out this could mean the bathroom needed toilet paper, the laundry needed to be moved from the washer to the dryer, she was about to mop the floor, she wanted permission to enter the kids' rooms, or we needed more Pledge—and could Esmeralda go through Pledge!

After a few months of working for us, she began accepting my offer to drive her to the bus stop in the afternoon. At first, I drove her to the stop closest to the house; eventually, I ended up driving her to the stop that allowed her to avoid two of her three cross-town buses. It was during these times she started talking to me. Always in Spanish, and always at a pace that matched the way she moved during the day—*fast*. This meant I heard about every third word and tried to fill in the rest using context clues.

On an afternoon in February, as we drove through town, Esmeralda said to me, "*No volveré. Me voy a América.*" She stared straight ahead. She was quiet.

My mind raced, trying to access my mental version of Google Translate. I had heard "*voy a América,*" which I knew meant "I am going to America." And *volveré* was likely some conjugated future tense of *volver* or "to return" (I am terrible at conjugating verbs). My mind finally clicked the words into place. *Wait, what? Esmeralda would not return. She was going to America.*

Esmeralda explained she was going to pay someone to take her across the border illegally. With tears in her eyes, she talked about her sons, eight and ten years old, whom she would leave in Oaxaca with her mother and sisters. I was amazed. I had no idea she had children. Esmeralda told me the job she had with us was the best job she had. We were the only family who treated her well. She said she saw no future for her or her sons in Mexico and had to try to make a better life for them. Esmeralda would leave the next day. She would try to get the boys to America soon.

I listened to Esmeralda in amazement. *Was she really telling me all of this? Did I really understand her?* It seemed like some sort of miracle in my Spanish language processing because I understood every word she said to me. My mind reeled.

What's my responsibility as an American knowing she's going to try to cross the border?

Did I play a role in her decision, by treating her with dignity and respect?

What risks is she taking?

Would she be hurt, detained, or worse—end up in the back of an eighteen-wheeler dead from heat exposure?

I didn't know much about Esmeralda, and I had so many questions I couldn't answer.

And her boys. How much desperation must she feel to decide to leave her children behind?

I couldn't possibly understand all the factors that went into Esmeralda's decision. But looking at Esmeralda, one mother to another, I knew this was not a decision she was making lightly. She knew the risks and was aware of the sacrifice, yet viewed America as the option to make enough money to give her boys an education and opportunity. To give them a better way of life. That I could understand. I want that for my children as well.

As I slowed to the corner where I would say goodbye to Esmeralda, I knew my responsibility at that moment was not to try to talk her out of her decision. It was not to try to protect America from a woman who only wanted to make a difference for her children. It was not to apply my lens to her situation. My responsibility was to see her as the proud, determined, and slightly scared woman who sat beside me. Taking her hand, I wished her the best of luck. She stepped out of my truck, onto her bus, and was gone.

I returned home with dusk settling around me, thinking about all that had transpired during my thirty-minute ride into the city. I felt different. Exposed, vulnerable, and sad. Before dinner that evening, I hugged my children tightly. We talked about Esmeralda's decision. Zane was initially indignant I hadn't tried to stop her, as he worried about her safety. Emily wondered how Esmeralda would make it in America—if she was able to get there—with her lack of English. Quinn worried about her sons. Bill was a quiet observer. We talked about how lucky we were to be together and blessed we were privileged not to have to make such a decision.

We talked about our view of Oaxaca, colorful and vibrant, versus Esmeralda's view where she felt trapped without opportunity. In the end, we explored our feelings and hers, knowing we could never truly understand all she was experiencing, but collectively came to the same place I had come to on the side of the road. We would support her, say a prayer, and wish her luck. I don't know if Esmeralda made it to America or not. But it was her road to walk. We could walk near her, but her shoes would never really fit us.

CHAPTER SIXTEEN

THE WHITE BOARD

Our whole life is solving puzzles.
—ERNO RUBIK, INVENTOR OF RUBIK'S CUBE

"I need a whiteboard. A big one," I said as I burst through the kitchen door into the mid-morning sunlight of the patio. It was 9:30 a.m. Bill and the kids were sitting in the shade of the umbrella eating lunch or what would have been lunch in Virginia even though it was only an hour later at home. *Sidebar question... Why is lunch always so early in middle school? It just seems wrong.*

I made my announcement with a bit of desperation and no small amount of urgency. The truck keys were in my hand as I reached for my shoes. "You need a whiteboard, right now? What's going on?" asked Bill. His line of questioning seemed preposterous to me because the need was crystal clear in my mind. Having to explain myself would only slow down my pursuit.

I had taken to working on the "what to do with my life" challenge at our breakfast table. I created a structure, whereby every morning I would assume my seat and begin working on my problem. Old habits of having a job and a set schedule die hard. My work consisted of reading books on leadership and personal growth—Brené Brown, Simon Sinek, Adam Grant, Bill Burnett, Carol Dweck, Oliver Burkeman, Clayton Christensen, Angela Duckworth—and taking notes. Lots and lots of notes. On lots and lots of sticky paper. I plastered the sticky notes all over the table, walls, and windows of the breakfast nook.

I started to see connections across my sticky notes when I sat down that morning. Dots were coming together, and a picture was forming. *Servant leadership. Helping people. Making a difference.* I had a primal need to synthesize my observations, write them down on a wall, step back, and look at my connections to see if the picture was clearer. I imagine this is why cavemen started writing on walls. The whiteboard: our modern-day cave drawings.

I didn't have time to explain myself further. I jumped into our truck and off I went to Staples. Yup, we had a Staples in town. Until this point, I had generally avoided it in favor of the local *tiendas* and *mercados*. They sold almost everything we could need. But I hadn't seen a whiteboard during any of my shopping trips. Staples seemed like my best option.

I arrived at Staples and lapped the store looking for my beloved whiteboard. I saw notebooks and pens, poster board and boxes, and at the very back corner of the store, an endcap with dry-erase markers. Bingo! I looked around but didn't see any whiteboards.

Shit. They don't have them.

I was dejected and about to head back home when I spied something shiny and white. It was tucked beneath a shelf, buried behind boxes and rolls of bubble wrap. *That might be it.* Like a treasure hunter who glimpses a treasure chest, I began digging, pulling out the items that surrounded my prize. Within moments a store clerk approached me, a bit wary of the frenetic, blonde *gringa* tearing apart the store.

"*¿Puedo ayudarle?* (Can I help you?)," he asked in a friendly manner, although it was clear he was worried about me.

"*No gracias. Estoy bien*," I replied with a smile while I continued digging so I could reach my prize. The clerk's facial expression revealed he thought I was anything but *fine*. I was unfazed. I had reached my beloved whiteboard. I pulled it out past the bubble wrap and boxes I had strewn across the floor; don't worry, I cleaned up the mess I had created. The whiteboard was covered in dust. I must have been one of the few to need a whiteboard in a long time. No matter. I had found my whiteboard. Mission accomplished.

I'm a visual learner. Drawings, doodles, and visual notes create a picture that words alone sometimes fail to convey. Doing the work to figure out what was next wasn't a linear process. Rather, it was a winding path that started and stopped—a path where I simultaneously had to look back to see where I'd been, look down to make sure I didn't trip, and look ahead to create a new path. I discovered clues along the way that helped me to move forward: clarified values, the kind of leader I wanted to be, and what was getting in my way—both the obstacles I created for myself and more systemic ones. And once I saw a mismatch in my values and other obstacles, I couldn't unsee them and knew I had to work to create alignment and remove the obstacles when possible. These clues were trail markers guiding me to a still yet unknown destination.

Clutching my giant whiteboard, I smiled with deep satisfaction and headed to the checkout counter. The store clerk returned my smile with a slight chuckle and what appeared to be an eye roll. *Loco American*, is what I can only assume he was thinking.

CHAPTER SEVENTEEN
ASKING FOR HELP

*Always give without remembering and
always receive without forgetting.*
—BRIAN TRACY

"Mom! Get the truck! We wrecked our bikes. Dad's hurt! We called an ambulance." Zane was standing on the balcony overlooking the garden and the pool. He was sweaty and covered in dirt. I stared up at him. My brain was working a beat or two slower than normal trying to take in what he had just said.

Shit! This isn't the plan. Our one rule for Mexico was no one was to get hurt or sick. We'd been warned about the quality, or lack thereof, of the healthcare system. We purchased supplemental international medical insurance because it seemed prudent, not because we were supposed to need it. So of course, within the first month of arriving in Oaxaca, Bill and Zane had taken up extreme mountain bike riding.

"Mom," Zane pleaded. From the pool deck below, I looked up at Zane. He'd grown several inches since we arrived and was now taller than me, but at that moment he looked small and scared. I took a deep breath to steady myself.

"Okay, buddy. Let me get the keys and a few things," I said. *Think, Suzanne. What do you need? Insurance cards. Bill's passport. Money—how much? Just grab all the pesos. The cell phone. Oh, thank God, I wasn't already swimming with the girls. Drying off would take way too long. Damn, the girls.*

Emily and Quinn were in the water on pool floats. They looked equally terrified. "Stay here. I mean get out of the pool, and stay here," I said. "I'm gonna take the cell phone, and I'll call the house phone as soon as I know anything." I found it interesting I could project some level of calm and control to the kids because on the inside I was scared and felt powerless. I guess this was true parenting.

"*Señor* Abdías! I need help, *por favor!*" I shouted to our landlord who was somewhere in the garden tending to the plants or peacocks. He didn't speak much English, so I have no idea why I yelled in English, but he felt like the only lifeline available to me at that moment.

"*¿Sí?*" he asked as his head, shaded by his ever-present, wide-brimmed sun hat, popped out from behind a large, red bougainvillea bush.

I explained, as best as I could, Bill was in an accident and was hurt. I needed to know which hospital we should go to since Oaxaca had COVID and non-COVID hospitals, public and private hospitals. *Señor* Abdías hurried into the house and up the stairs still carrying the machete he'd been using in the garden. I followed.

At the top of the stairs was a small table with an old rotary phone on it. Until this point, the phone had been a novelty item. "You had to remember phone numbers?" and "It took this long to dial?" and "You couldn't walk around; you were stuck with the cord?" the kids had asked. Bill and I had replied, "Yes, times were hard way back in the '90s."

Señor Abdías took my hands, "*Tranquila, tranquila, tranquila.*" Calm. It seemed my fear was shining through to *Señor* Abdías. Then he dropped to his knees and began dialing the phone. He dialed more nines than should exist in any one phone number. He shoved his index finger into the dial holes. I heard a *swoosh* as the dial rotated toward the finger stop and a *click-click-click* as the dial returned to its starting position. It was excruciatingly slow!

"*Señor,*" I said, holding my cell phone out. *Surely the cell phone had to be faster.* But he waved it away. After what seemed like an eternity, he began speaking to someone. He hung up the phone and turned to me.

"*Hospital San José en Reforma. Es privado y bueno,*" he said, standing up with the machete still in his hand. He awkwardly embraced me because of the machete. "It will be all right," *Señor* Abdías said in English looking me in the eyes. I felt more confident. I had the name of the hospital. It was a good one. That would have to do for now. This time I grabbed *Señor* Abdías in a tight hug. Thanked him, called for Zane, and sprinted for the truck.

Thankfully, Bill crashed his mountain bike only a few streets away from our house. I drove as fast as I could but was stopped by Oaxacan road work. Standing between Bill and I was a giant hole in the street at least fifty feet across and twenty-five feet deep. It hadn't been there the day before.

"What do we do?" I asked, sort of to Zane but more to myself. I leaned forward, resting my forearms on the steering wheel, assessing the situation and trying to figure out a plan. I couldn't get the truck around this hole. In the rearview mirror, I saw a flash of lights as the ambulance pulled up behind me. *What took them so long? Why aren't they already with Bill? Even ambulances work slower here.*

The ambulance driver surveyed the road situation. He looked perplexed. He and another EMT exchanged words I didn't understand at a rapid pace. The driver looked at the hole, then at Zane and me, shrugged his shoulders, and walked back to the ambulance. It seemed like the EMTs were giving up. Bill was at least a quarter mile on the other side of this hole. He needed help and we had no way to get to him.

"*¡Hola! ¡Espérame!* (Hello! Wait for me!)," yelled a young man. He was running toward us, skirting along the side of the hole. He waved at us and the EMTs. "I can show you how to get around the hole." He yelled something to the ambulance driver and jumped into the truck. "Hi. Turn the truck around; we need to take the long way to get to Bill," he said. I was frozen. He spoke impeccable English, without any trace of an accent. It seemed like he had just arrived from Virginia and climbed into my truck, but we were in Oaxaca. As he buckled his seatbelt he said, "Bill is okay; he is conscious. *¡Vámonos*, let's go! It's a ten-minute drive."

The ambulance followed me at a snail's pace around turns, over bumps, and through the hillside neighborhood of San Felipe del Agua. *No wonder it takes them so long to get anywhere.* I stopped the truck where the street met the footpath that took you up the mountain. Bill was lying in the middle of the dirt road surrounded by people from the neighborhood. A woman wiped his forehead with a washcloth. He was covered in dirt and a white blanket covered his legs (before my arrival, the blanket had been pulled up to his chin, but Bill had instructed the neighbors to pull the blanket down when I arrived so I wouldn't freak out thinking he was dead).

"Hey. Are you okay?" I asked softly, choking back tears and kneeling beside Bill to take his hand. Seeing he was alert calmed my nerves a bit.

"Yeah," he said in short breaths. "Might be a broken rib. Can't breathe. Maybe a punctured lung." And with that, the paramedics pushed me out of the way and began tending to Bill. I stumbled backward from where Bill lay to the outer circle where the neighbors and bystanders stood. A woman took hold of my shaking hand, and I reached for Zane with my other. I felt helpless wondering what this injury would mean for Bill and our family.

The rest of the day proceeded in somewhat of a blur. I recall the overwhelming kindness of strangers who didn't have to help us, who didn't have to care but did. A woman stood between Zane and I holding both of our hands, offering us water and reassurances Bill would be all right.

The boisterous neighbors, talking over one another and yelling at the paramedics, voicing their opinions about which hospital Bill should be taken to, finally settled on the hospital *Señor* Abdías had recommended.

The older gentleman, dressed in a down winter coat and sandals, broke a sweat helping me load the mountain bikes into the truck so I could take them home before going to the hospital. *The only thing that would have upset Bill more than his injury would have been if the bikes were stolen.*

And Esteban, who was riding with Bill and Zane when they wrecked, jumped into the ambulance with Bill so he wouldn't be alone, stayed with us at the hospital for hours to translate so I would understand the doctors, and his dad brought us dinner as our time in the hospital dragged on.

In Oaxaca, the word *guelaguetza* is derived from the Zapotec dialect. It loosely translates in English to an offering or reciprocity. Guelaguetza is the name of an annual cultural exchange celebration and the way life is lived. In times of celebration, struggles, happiness, or need, *Oaxaqueños* share what they have with others, no matter how much or how little. The receiver is expected to accept the offering with an open heart and the knowledge they will one day return the favor (País n.d.).

I am not good at asking for things—hell, I hate making a reservation at a restaurant because I don't want to bother people—and I am not good at asking for help. I prefer to try to keep things within my control. However, that day I could control very little. When I needed to surrender, trust, and put my faith in others, I discovered the beauty that underlies the spirit of Guelaguetza.

I witnessed the best in others, in Zane, and in myself. I was able to recognize all that was good in the situation: Bill was near our home when he crashed, not far off in the mountains; the exact spot where Bill lay in the street waiting for the ambulance to arrive was usually covered in running sewage water, but the water had been turned off because of the roadwork; although he had torn the cartilage from his ribs and was battered and bruised (fifty-year-old bodies don't bounce) his injuries were relatively minor compared to the initial suspicion of broken ribs and a punctured lung. The care he received was much better (and cheaper) than we had expected.

Most importantly, I realized people wanted to help us. Whether I asked or not, these strangers showed up and were there for us. They didn't know us. They didn't have to help, but they did. Generally, people like to help other people. I like helping other people. It is what I love doing most. So why does my desire for control, or at least to appear to be in control, override the knowledge people like helping others? Helping people allows you to make connections. Asking for help exposes your vulnerability and lets you get closer to people.

That day, I saw again how when the control was taken away, I was at my best in making connections with others. Although I wish Bill didn't have to get hurt to remind me of the power of vulnerability and connections, I am grateful I was able to connect in a meaningful way with my neighbors that day. I am grateful for their help and will be there to return the favor one day.

CHAPTER EIGHTEEN

IDENTITY

We know what we are, but not what we may be.
—OPHELIA, HAMLET BY WILLIAM SHAKESPEARE

"*¿Qué haces para trabajar en los Estados Unidos?* (What do you do for work in the United States?)," our neighbor Federico asked as we sat by his outdoor fireplace, relaxing after dinner. It was a cool evening, the moon was full, and our children, six of them, were running through the garden playing hide and seek—a universal game that transcends language barriers.

Staring into the fire, I pondered Federico's question. It was simple, one I had answered a thousand times before. This question was subject to jokes and a certain measure of disdain in the Washington, DC area because the response is mainly used as a way to size up the relative power of the other person. "I work on Capitol Hill," "I'm at the White House," or my personal favorite, "I'm with the government. How about this weather we're having?" (I have found this answer to be code for, "I'm in a classified role and would need to kill you if I told you what I do, so don't ask."). In Oaxaca, however, the question of *what do you do?* seemed to be one of sincere interest. Exploring why we were there, how we could afford so much time away from our lives, and what we were interested in.

I stumbled in my attempt to answer Federico. Part of my hesitation was I didn't have all the words in Spanish to formulate a coherent answer. Despite spending hours studying Spanish every week, it was difficult to engage in a meaningful and connective conversation. I was sure my "Spanglish" was at best amusing, at worst offensive, and most likely just downright annoying.

Federico recognized I was struggling and kindly said, "*Tome su tiempo.* (Take your time)." He rose and began fiddling with the logs on the fire. I was exhausted, and my face revealed it. It took so much effort and focus to engage for an entire evening in Spanish. But more than words, the question itself was something I'd been pondering quite a bit. *What did I do?* I wasn't sure I had the answer these days.

If I had been at a cocktail party or networking event in the United States, my standard answer would have been, "I am a partner at a management consulting firm." In my mind being a partner was less about what I did and more about who I was. It was my measure of worth and importance. It was how I received immediate feedback and the quick dopamine hit that comes from positive praise. Being a partner was my identity. And yet, in trying to answer the question *what was next for me?* I had to wrestle with the fact if what was next wasn't in management consulting, then I wouldn't be a partner. And if I wasn't a partner at the firm, then who was I?

I had been captivated by the idea of working for a management consulting firm since my freshman year at Syracuse University. In the spring of 1993, I was considering applying to the business school when a simple conversation with my roommate's brother Darren, a senior majoring in accounting, cemented my decision.

We were somewhere on the Pennsylvania Turnpike driving back to Syracuse. Everything was dull. The road was gray from the still common in this part of northeast Pennsylvania long into March. The sky was dark with heavy clouds that hung low. The car, a dirt-streaked Chevy Cavalier, signaled it belonged to a college student who would rather spend money on beer than on a car wash. And the conversation—we'd been driving for almost two hours and hadn't said more than three sentences to each other. I couldn't take the awkwardness anymore. "So Melanie tells me you are an accounting major. How do you like it?" I asked as I rubbed my hands together. I was at once nervous to interrupt the silence and cold because the heat wasn't working.

"It's good," he said flatly. "It's more interesting than a lot of people think. There are lots of internships and jobs available once you graduate. You can earn a bunch of money, like thirty thousand dollars a year. Lots of firms come to campus for recruiting. All the Big Six, you know, like Arthur Andersen, Coopers & Lybrand, Deloitte, Ernst &

Young, KPMG, Pricewaterhouse. And a bunch of smaller firms too," he trailed off.

It was an innocuous conversation, merely meant to break the awkward silence, but Darren's comments piqued my interest. I wish I could tell you exactly what it was about accounting and management consulting that seemed interesting. Perhaps I saw it as a way to get a job in a city. Perhaps I was impressed by what sounded like a ridiculous amount of money to my eighteen-year-old self. Perhaps I made the connection with my uncle who had been a partner at an accounting firm and lived in Belgium. Accounting might be my ticket to the world. Or perhaps it was simply what seemed like a checklist to success: an accounting degree, plus an internship, plus a full-time job, equaled success. Whatever it was, Darren's off-the-cuff response set me on a path to whom I had become.

And now, over twenty-five years later, I was in Oaxaca struggling to reinvent myself. I thought about the motivators I had when I was in my twenties and thirties: achievement, personal mastery, and financial reward. But as I rounded the bend into my late forties, I found my motivators had changed. I was driven now by my desire to help others, to be of service, and to make a difference on both a large and small scale.

What did this change in motivators mean for my identity that had previously been defined by achievement?

Try as I might, I couldn't figure this out for myself. So I enrolled in the Hudson Institute of Coaching's

LifeForward program, which is billed as an intensive four-day experience designed to "let participants press 'pause' in their busy lives and explore how life has unfolded up until now and contemplate how they would like to consciously shift and reshape elements of life going forward" (Hudson Institute 2022).

Yes, please, I thought when I read the program description. Little did I know just how transformative this experience would be.

On day one of LifeForward, I settled in with nine other strangers across a Zoom screen. We shared our life stories, the good and the bad. We laughed and cried together, and within three hours, we were bonded to one another. Our facilitator introduced the concept of life chapters and the cycles of renewal adults experience. We experience a phase of firing on all cylinders, chasing your goals, and striving to do more; a phase where you plateau and feel a bit bored and restless; a phase where you reinvent yourself, experiment with new roles and a new sense of self; and a phase where you look inward and ask big questions about who you are and who you wanted to be. This phase is called cocooning (Hudson 1999).

I was squarely in cocooning. But here was the thing, according to our facilitator: to move out of the cocooning phase you may need to let go of your identity and the sense of self that had been holding you back. Cocooning is where deep inner work and transformation happens. Moving forward required you to recognize what you were giving up, acknowledge the loss, and grieve the person you once were. Without doing this, people could get stuck in this phase and not move forward (Hudson 1999).

Boom! That was it. If I wanted to figure out who I was going to be and what I was supposed to be doing, I needed to let go of the identity I had created for myself. The one that started to form when I was eighteen and was now solidly embedded in my view of myself—I was only a partner in a management consulting firm. This realization quite literally took my breath away. I stopped talking mid-sentence and was silent. It was as if the fog had lifted and I could see a path forward. Not an answer, but a path. I was overcome with emotion, and my face and the tears welling in my eyes must have shown it (I do not have a poker face) because I immediately received a chat message from one of my co-participants that said, "I don't know what just happened for you, but whatever it was, it must have been big. I am here for you."

It was big. At that moment I realized what I do and who I am are not the same thing. I am many things: a wife, a friend, a mother, an expert on compliance issues, a pretty good cook, an empath, a great listener, a process improver, a creative, funny, sensitive, a crier—clearly, I cry a lot—a hard worker, and I just happen to have a job as a partner in a management consulting firm. Whether I decided to stay with the firm or leave, being a partner would always be part of my resume, but it was not who I am.

Back by the glow of the fire, I looked at Federico and proceeded to explain my interests in art and reading, in continuously learning and exploring new cultures, in cooking, and in my newfound passion for mezcal. We chatted about his interests in horse riding, golf, wine, and starting an oyster farm (I wasn't expecting that one). Not once did I mention I was a partner at a management consulting firm. I didn't know where I was going exactly, but I was figuring out who I am. And even in my broken Spanish, I am a pretty interesting person.

CHAPTER NINETEEN

STUFF

> *When you lose your desire for things
> that do not matter, you will be free.*
> —MORIHEI UESHIBA

Scroll. Click. Buy it now.

Dish soap. *Click.* Socks. *Click.* Tapered candles shaped like corn on the cob—required for Thanksgiving, of course. *Click.*

I used to jolt awake in the middle of the night with the anxiety and stress of my job pressing upon my chest. I wouldn't be able to sleep. But rather than worry, I would grab my phone and do some midnight shopping by the cold, blue light of websites. I assumed I was being productive and efficient. The convenience of online shopping can't be beaten.

Packages would arrive on my doorstep in a day or two. Some days, three or four boxes would arrive at a time, but by then, I'd have no idea what was in them. It would take opening the boxes to see what was inside. *Oh yeah, I remember ordering this.*

This begs the question, did I really "need" most of the stuff I ordered? The case of twenty-four mini-disco balls? Yup, this was an actual purchase I once made. To be clear, for an entire year, we gave mini-disco balls to neighborhood kids as birthday gifts. They were a huge hit. So maybe that purchase was a necessity.

But did I need all the stuff I ordered? I thought I did. To be fair, dish soap and socks are important. But eventually, the stuff began to feel overwhelming and suffocating. Like it was taking over every inch of our house. I swear the plastic toys kids receive in party goody bags or fast-food meals seemed to reproduce in the dead of night. Even when I threw them away, these toys somehow ended up back in the house again. It was maddening, but I didn't know how to stop my impulse to click and buy more stuff.

And the stuff ended up everywhere, always out of place. I found a term that perfectly described the state of stuff in our house when the Smithsonian's Renwick Museum held an exhibit featuring photography and art installations from Burning Man. I've always been intrigued by the concept of Burning Man, and part of me wants to go, but I am afraid I am not enough of a free spirit. If you haven't been to or heard of Burning Man, it is an annual event to celebrate self-expression, connection, and community (Burning Man 2022). Every year in the Black Rock Desert of Nevada, an entire self-sufficient city is built, celebrated, and destroyed. Burning Man is so unique it even has its own vocabulary. My favorite term is MOOP or Matter Out of Place (Burning Man 2022).

I adopted the term MOOP as my own after I saw it at the Renwick. When all our stuff becomes overwhelming and slightly suffocating, I go on a MOOP run. I gather up the MOOP and place it in a central location announcing, "There's MOOP in the kitchen. I set a timer. If your MOOP isn't put away within fifteen minutes, I'm throwing it in the trash." MOOP announcements work like a charm to get people to clean up the messes that have been strewn about the house. If you think it will work for you, go ahead and steal the trick. As the kids say, #lifehack.

Online, convenience shopping didn't really exist in Oaxaca. Shopping was never a click of a button or a quick in and out of a store. It was more like an adventurous treasure hunt! Sometimes you wouldn't even be looking for something but would just happen to find it. One day I was in the big box grocery store, and there before me in the "*gringo* aisle" were Thomas' Bagels. We'd missed bagels. They were a big hit.

But most days shopping was a decision tree. What did we want or need? Where might I find it: local *mercado*, corner *tienda*, or superstores like a grocery store or Walmart? Did they have it? If they didn't have it, was a substitute available? And when all else failed and you needed something obscure, could you purchase it on Mercado Libre? Mercado Libre was the Mexican version of Amazon, and it was a process. Allow me to explain.

We had a pool at our house, and every few days Felix would come to clean and manage the chlorine levels. And when I say manage the chlorine levels, I mean he would dump copious amounts of chlorine powder into the water. So it was no surprise within a few weeks of arriving, Emily and Quinn's hair started turning green. (I avoided green hair because I either refused to put my head underwater or wore a swim cap.)

So off I went looking for a shampoo to remove the chlorine-green color from the girls' hair. My first mistake was wandering the aisles of Walmart looking for shampoo specifically for people with *blonde* hair. I am not sure how I failed to notice Oaxaca was in a sea of people who had predominantly dark hair. A minor discoloration from chlorine was not likely to cause a problem.

My second mistake was asking a young woman wearing a Walmart uniform and stocking the shelves with hair care products if they carried shampoo specifically for blondes. She looked at me like I was insane. I left Walmart and moved on to option number two: finding a substitute.

A quick search on Google told me baking soda and lemon juice could remove chlorine green from hair. Bingo! *But where do I find baking soda?* I hadn't seen the little yellow Arm & Hammer boxes anywhere. "Every corner *tienda* sells baking soda," said Chris as we were sitting at the table on the veranda, and I was attempting to conjugate verbs. Chris was not only my Spanish teacher but also my teacher on the ways things got done in Oaxaca and my friend.

I walked to the corner *tienda* at the end of our street. I looked around, no yellow boxes. I asked. Baking soda was kept behind the counter and sold by weight. Next challenge...how many grams did I need? And how much is a gram anyway? The stupid US and our refusal to adopt the metric system!

The woman behind the counter had no patience for my indecision and gave me a sandwich baggie full of baking soda. "*Nueve* (nine) *pesos*," said the clerk holding out her hands. Mere pennies and my green hair problem would be solved. I was hopeful. We applied the mixture of baking soda and lemon juice. We still had green hair.

My next and final option was to buy swimmers shampoo from Mercado Libre. At a minimum, it was a ten-step process.

Step one: Create an account on Mercado Libre.

Step two: Find what you are looking for in a sea of unfamiliar Mexican products.

Step three: Order what you want.

Step four: Record your order confirmation code.

Step five: Drive to the OXXO (the Mexican 7-11), present your order confirmation code, and pay for your order in cash.

Step six: Remember to get the payment confirmation code from OXXO. Don't lose it.

Step seven: Drive home.

Step eight: Log back into your Mercado Libre account and enter your payment confirmation code.

Step nine: Enter your delivery information and submit the order.

Step ten: Wait for the postal service to deliver your package, which may or may not happen.

I used to click "Buy Now" in the middle of the night without a second thought. The complexities to buy something from Mercado Libre made me stop and think. And think really hard. *Did I really need what I was looking for? Was I willing to go through the hassle?* Aside from the shampoo, we largely found we could do without the stuff we thought we needed. The shampoo didn't work anyway, so we embraced the green hair. It was what we had, and it was all good.

It was liberating to not have so much stuff. We figured out how to make do. I resisted the urge to shop as a way to kill time or avoid other things on my mind. I discovered I liked it. We had less MOOP in the house because we just didn't have that much stuff. I could breathe!

Above all, it made us all appreciate what we had and what we could find. Quinn made a horse stable out of a cardboard box and construction paper to play with. One day she asked if she could buy some toy horses to put into the stable. We found a toy store that sold plastic horse figurines, but they only had a Pegasus and a knight with his steed. Quinn bought them and ripped the wings off the Pegasus and crafted saddles out of fabric and glue; she named the horses Teddy and Blue. After we returned to the US, Quinn got several more horses and a large, plastic stable. While putting her to bed one night, I asked, "Out of all of these horses, who are your favorites?"

Without hesitation, Quinn reached for the two horses that looked different from the rest. "Teddy and Blue," she said. "They're the 'OGs.' The *Oaxaca Gangstas*. They were my only toys there. They're special."

It's amazing how quickly human beings can adapt. About two months after we arrived, we had the opportunity to visit friends in Mexico City, who were able to get shipments from Amazon more easily than we were able to. Before our visit, my friend sent me a note asking if I wanted them to order anything for us. I will admit, my heart raced a little at the idea of being able to get almost anything I desired. I hustled to my computer and launched Amazon's website. I stared at the screen in front of me for a while. A bit perplexed, I honestly couldn't think of a single thing we needed. I was free.

I picked up my phone and texted my girlfriend, "Nothing needed from Amazon. We're good."

And that may have been an understatement.

CHAPTER TWENTY

HUMMINGBIRD

Take delight in the small things in life.
The sweetest nectar you will find is within you.
—ANONYMOUS

"*Eres un colibrí.* (You are a hummingbird)," said Anjélico Jimenéz.

Anjélico is a third generation Zapotec artisan. The Zapotecs are one of several indigenous cultures in Mexico that date back to pre-Columbian times. Within Zapotec culture, it is believed each person has a *tona*, an animal or a protective spirit guide assigned to each person based on their birthday on the Zapotec calendar. Artisans, such as Anjélico, carve and intricately paint beautiful wooden *alebrijes* to represent these *tonas*. I am a hummingbird.

"Come on guys," I said to the kids standing in the doorway to Zane's bedroom. Zane was on the computer playing video games, Quinn was on the iPad watching YouTube, and Emily was on Snapchat on her phone. "You have the day off from school. We're not sitting inside all day. We're going on an adventure. Off the devices. Let's go."

It was election day 2020, and for several days Emily and Zane had been talking about watching the election results all day. Although I had to admire their budding interest in politics, I knew they would be bored with the talking heads of the cable news networks by mid-morning, resulting in more video games and a TikTok marathon for the rest of the day. *Not on my watch.* It was a beautiful fall day. We were going to visit two of the artisan *pueblos* on the outskirts of Oaxaca de Juarez.

In the short time we had been in Oaxaca, I discovered each artisan town was seemingly dedicated to a single craft: the *alebrije* towns of Arrazola and San Martin Tilcajete, the black pottery town of San Bartolo Coyotepec, San Antonino is the embroidery town, and Teotitlán del Valle is the rug town.

"Let's go," I said again to the grumbles of three kids who were not thrilled with my plan. I didn't care about their complaints. I was excited to get out and explore. "First we're going to Santa Maria Atzompa," I announced as I cheerily gathered my purse. "It's the green pottery town. Then we'll go to Arrazola. I hope we can paint *alebrijes*."

I had plotted out our trip the night before using GPS, and the directions were straightforward. The map showed it to be just over seven miles from our house to the "green pottery" town, another six miles to the *alebrije* town, and about thirteen miles home. It looks like a perfect triangle. Simple. *The GPS lied!*

Getting to Atzompa was easy, although traveling seven miles in Oaxaca takes about fifty minutes. Getting from Atzompa to Arrazola was a different story. It was anything but easy.

"The GPS says to make the next left," Zane said. He was my co-pilot providing me warnings of the upcoming turns, as I was still nervous navigating the streets of Oaxaca.

"Are you sure? That's a cornfield. We need to go over the mountain," I said, trying to glance at the map while navigating the road.

"It's what it says," he replied, with a tone that suggested, *Do you want a co-pilot or not, lady?*

I reluctantly made the turn into the cornfield and away from civilization. The path before us zigged and zagged, but we were gaining elevation, so maybe we would head over the mountain to our destination after all. Zane continued to feed me directions in advance of "Miss Direction"—our name for our GPS voice. Soon enough we exited the cornfield and returned to a paved road, which was a relief.

Things seemed to be going well, a little slower than I had expected, the route a little more remote than I anticipated, but we were making progress. That is until the road ended abruptly. It was not like the paved road stopped and a dirt road continued; that would have been expected. Nope, the road just ended in a stand of trees with barely enough room to turn around. I turned to Zane with a questioning expression.

"Don't ask me," he said as he zoomed out on the GPS map. "On here the road continues. But then again, we may have lost signal back there, so you never know."

"Okay," I said with a drawl that extended the word and conveyed my dismay.

After making a seventeen-point turn, we retraced our path down the mountain, through the cornfield, and back to civilization. We turned away from the mountain; if we couldn't go over it, we'd go around it. I wouldn't be deterred by a road that ended at the top of a mountain. Looking back, I should have been. That paved road with its beautiful view of the valley below should have been the highlight of our adventure.

Onward, we bounced down dirt roads, between massive potholes and through places where the road had washed away. After driving for an hour and a half, we came to a wooden bridge that had collapsed leaving the twenty-foot span over a dried riverbed impassable. The car was quiet. My stomach was growling. It was long past lunchtime. *We should have stopped at the pizza place back there.* The kids had to be hungry as well. The wheels in my head spun as I considered our options.

Should I keep going? To where exactly? This is nuts. You have limited cell service, and the GPS is clearly broken. Admit it, Suzanne, you are lost. This trip is a bust. Go home before something really bad happens. Alebrijes aren't in the cards today. The condescending voice of responsibility in my head was on its soapbox. My resolve to get to Arrazola faltered. We needed to abort the mission.

As I was about to tell the kids we were heading home, the confident voice of Miss Direction broke the silence announcing, "In eight hundred feet, make a left turn and your destination will be on the right."

Is she kidding me? We were in the middle of nowhere. A giant hole is in front of us, some goats and a cow to our right, another corn field to our left, and what appears to be a tin shack with a rusty Modelo beer sign across the abyss. And Miss Direction thinks we were almost there?

Overcome by the absurdity of the situation, I began to laugh. What started as a giggle soon turned into a wild, belly laugh with tears rolling down my face and my breathing choked into gasps. The kids looked at me like I had lost my mind.

"Oh no, there she goes," said Zane. "We've lost her." They looked at one another and broke into hysterics that rivaled mine.

When we regained our composure, I said, "What do you want to do?"

Zane chimed in first, "Miss Direction says we are almost there. She hasn't been wrong at all today. Let's go." He was energetic, confident, and a tad bit sarcastic. He had a little twinkle in his eye as he knew we would have to go off-roading for a bit. So we persevered.

And do you know what? Miss Direction was not broken. For once that day, she was right. After we made our way around the collapsed bridge, we passed through another cornfield and the town of Arrazola emerged. After another few turns, we arrived.

Anjélico's workshop was filled with *alibrijes* of all kinds. Powerful jaguars, majestic deer, imposing bulls, and a variety of other fierce spirit protectors. Each is painted in vibrant colors and traditional Zapotec patterns. He welcomed us in and motioned for us to follow him into the back room.

"Each *alibrije* starts from the wood of the copal tree. We soak the wood in water to soften it and carve it into the animal we are looking for. Once the wood is completely dry, we can paint it. It can take between four months to a year to carve and paint a medium to large-sized *alibrije*," Anjélico said as he reached for a weathered notebook. "Tell me your birthday, and I will tell you your Zapotec *tona*."

With each birthday provided, Anjélico flipped through his notebook, ran his finger down the paper, and announced our *tonas*. Emily and Zane were deer, the hunters. Bill was an armadillo, the protector; Quinn was a jaguar, the most revered animal in Zapotec culture. My family was aligned with some very strong and powerful *tonas*. So when Anjélico said, "*Señora*, you are a hummingbird," I admit I was not thrilled.

I mean who wants to have a tiny, delicate hummingbird as their spirit animal? Not me! First, I am afraid of birds; yes, I know it is irrational, but I have been attacked by multiple birds. I think they are shifty and unpredictable, and I just don't like them. Sorry to my bird friends. To be told my spirit protector was a hummingbird felt like some sort of cruel irony where the one protecting the prize is the one who is out to destroy it.

Second, hummingbirds are so small. I had imagined my protector would be strong and foreboding to guide me on this journey through life. I have always considered myself to be strong and consistent. I keep us together. *No way I am a hummingbird. I am the opposite of a hummingbird.*

"Within the Zapotec culture hummingbirds are considered symbols of good luck, bringing good intentions from one person to another, in both life and death. They represent light and joy. Hummingbirds lift others up to see the good and sweetness in life," Anjélico said as he pulled out several colorful hummingbird *alibrijes*. "From an evolutionary perspective, hummingbirds defy the laws of physics, flying forward, backward, and upside down. The hummingbird's wings are uniquely adapted making them the only species of birds that can hover in a single spot. They are incredibly agile with amazing speed and stamina. They are fierce protectors. That's why hummingbirds can travel between the living and the spirit world."

Contemplating Anjélico's description of the

hummingbird's symbolic and evolutionary traits, my initial outrage softened. Maybe my *tona* wasn't out to get me. Maybe I had judged too quickly. The hummingbird and I shared similarities. I am the one who sees the positive, laughing like crazy when lost on a dirt road. The one who is present for my family and friends. The one who defies expectations. The one who sees the good in people and situations. The one who is fierce and protective. And so, I am a hummingbird, and my *tona* is guiding me well through this life.

CHAPTER TWENTY-ONE
DELFINES

To have your childhood dream realized is a really big deal.
—MAYA RUDOLPH

"*Señor, rapido. Hey mucho delfines en este momento. Vamos.* (Sir, you must hurry. There are many dolphins right now. Let's go)," El Capitán said. He was running barefoot alongside our car, yelling into the open window while directing us to a parking spot ahead.

Eight of us tumbled out of the car and rushed across the beachfront street trying to keep El Capitán in our sites. His head bounced up and down. He seemed to be playing a game of hopscotch, jumping over and around the sunbathers as he crossed the beach. Stepping onto the beach, the sand was hot—like you could feel the heat radiate through your flip-flops hot. *How are people laying in the sand?* Within a few steps, I too was playing El Capitán's game. Jumping from spot to spot, I avoided the crowds of children and sunbathers and kept my feet moving so they wouldn't burn too badly in the hot sand.

The cool ocean was a welcome relief for my singed feet, and I took my time as I waded toward our boat. A wave of nausea passed over me as I caught sight of the small boat bouncing in the surf. *Please don't let me get seasick.* Two men attempted to hold the boat steady in the swimming cove, as they shoved the kids one by one into the boat. It was barely larger than the Boston Whaler my brother and I had puttered around on when we were kids. *Please let this boat be safe.*

A group of children played in the surf. I tasted salt as a boy dove into the water in front of me and transported me from my thoughts back to Puerto Escondido's swimming beach.

"*Rapido, señora,*" called one of the men who was trying to hold the boat steady. I stepped to the stern of the boat not entirely confident I was going to make it into the boat. I placed my foot on the engine block, and at that moment, a swell lifted the boat. I felt myself rising and with a push to my backside, I was catapulted over the stern wall into the boat. Not graceful, but effective.

"*Gracias,*" I said, trying to steady myself. Before I could get my sea legs about me, El Capitán jumped into the boat, started the engine, and gunned the throttle. The force of the boat's acceleration caused all of us to fall into the nearest seat. The boat sped through the cove with swimmers diving out of our path.

"So much for the safety briefing," Emily said ironically as she pulled herself from the floor of the boat, where she had landed when the boat took off, up onto the seat. "Keep your hands and feet inside the boat at all times during the ride."

Quinn sat next to Emily. Her legs were crossed, her foot was shaking, and she was nervously wringing a beach towel in her hands. "Where are the life jackets?" Quinn asked.

"You're funny, Quinnie," said Aliza. "I love how you assume there are life jackets. It's Mexico; just go with it." Aliza and her parents, who lived in Mexico City, had met us in Puerto for our beach week. Aliza had a dry wit and a keen perspective on how things were done in Mexico.

The boat accelerated until it was skimming across the clear blue waters of the Pacific Ocean. I took a quick headcount. Emily, Zane, Quinn, Aliza, Bill, Tom, Kimberly, and me were all present and accounted for. I tried to convince myself Aliza was being dramatic for effect. *The boat must have life jackets, right?*

"*Hay mucho delfines en ocho o doce millas,*" said El Capitán, talking to no one in particular. He was standing confidently at the helm looking at the horizon as if he could see where the dolphins were out there in the vast expanse of the sea.

"Kimberly, did he just say the dolphins are *eight to twelve miles* offshore?" I asked. Now I was really nervous. The boat was no more than twenty-five feet from bow to stern, a small fishing boat at best. It should not be heading twelve miles out to sea. And with the speed we were moving, I wasn't sure El Capitán was the one who should be taking us that far out. Between the roar of the engines and my poor Spanish, I must have misheard El Capitán.

Kimberly turned with a look of apprehension on her face. "Yeah, I heard that too." Surprise and panic rose within me. The theme song from *Gilligan's Island* popped into my head. *I didn't pack my evening gowns, and the boat doesn't have life jackets. This is suboptimal.*

For an hour we headed further and further away from shore. It was too loud to talk. We could only look at the water and sky. We bounced and skipped across the water. Each of us used one hand to hold onto the boat and the other to hold onto our hats. Every so often El Capitán would pull out the boat's radio, start talking to someone, and adjust our course. The relative silence and our unknown destination did nothing to relieve my anxiety.

Without warning the boat slowed, El Capitán made his way to the bow, and the first mate assumed the helm. Honestly, I hadn't seen the first mate until then; it seemed like he had appeared out of thin air. But he had to have been on the boat. It was so small he would've had no place to hide. El Capitán leaned over the bow of the boat, grabbed a line, and wrapped it around his hands. He assumed a stance, which oddly looked like he was riding a bull in bright orange swim trunks. He announced there were dolphins in two miles and he was going to look for them. The first mate gunned the engines again.

El Capitán held the rope in one hand and pointed to the horizon with the other. *These guys are nuts.*

"Oh my god! Look, look!" shouted Emily. She was standing, mouth agape, holding the brim of her baseball cap, and pointing at the horizon in wonder. It took a moment for the others to focus on where Emily was pointing. But once they did the boat was alive with screams of excitement.

Dolphins! At least ten dolphins could be seen silhouetted against the clear blue sky. They were jumping ten to fifteen feet into the air. They were the only thing you could see against the horizon. It was magnificent.

We approached the pod of dolphins and El Capitán cut the boat engine. "*Nos metemos y nadamos* (Jump in and swim)," instructed El Capitán.

We get to swim with the dolphins. This was twelve-year-old Suzanne's dream come true. As a kid, all I wanted was to be a dolphin trainer. I spent hours in the summer watching old reruns of *Flipper* and inventing imaginative games where I was Sandy, the kid from *Flipper,* and my dog played the role of Flipper the dolphin. I had a very active imagination. At one point I had visions of me working at the National Aquarium in Baltimore or at Sea World training dolphins.

And while swimming with dolphins was my childhood dream, the current situation was somewhat of a nightmare for adult Suzanne. We were twelve miles off the coast, I couldn't see the shore, and my kids had just jumped into the ocean, sans life jackets.

The kids were shrieking in delight, talking over one another. "Come on, Mom! Get in the water. You're gonna love it," shouted Zane as he broke the surface.

Quinn's head popped up. "When you go underwater you can hear the dolphins! It is amazing," Quinn exclaimed, and she disappeared beneath the water again. Over and over the kids' heads broke the surface before submerging again. They shrieked with delight. They were elated, but I was nervous.

I'd never seen so many dolphins at once; around two hundred of them surrounded the boat. We were in the middle of their pod. *What are you doing just standing here? Get in the water.*

"Do you have life jackets?" I asked, turning to El Capitán. The boat rolled gently over the waves. He reached under a seat and handed me a single, orange life vest. *One's better than none,* I reasoned as I threw the life jacket into the water.

Standing on the gunwale of the boat, I mustered the courage to put aside my adult fears and dove in. The water was oddly warm for being twelve miles offshore—more like a pool than the ocean. Instantly, I was surrounded by the sounds of the dolphins' squeaks, cries, and clicks. It was beyond twelve-year-old Suzanne's wildest imagination. The water swirled around my legs as dolphins swam past.

I broke the surface smiling broadly. I joined in with the shrieks of amazement with my kids.

Bill was holding onto a life jacket just outside of the circle of swimming kids (two more life vests had appeared by this point). Taking hold of the corner of the vest, I scanned the scene. A beautiful setting, and an amazing experience with the people I love most. Emily would later tell me our trip to the beach and swimming with the dolphins was her favorite experience in Mexico.

"I hope El Capitán doesn't take off and leave us stranded in the ocean," Bill said, interrupting my contemplation and bringing me back to the reality of our situation. We were still twelve miles offshore, with a person-to-life jacket ratio that wasn't great, and a boat slowly drifting away from us in the current.

"Yeah," I said with a small chuckle. "That would suck. It's a long swim." With that, I dunked my head underwater to listen to the songs of the dolphins. I felt like a kid again, free in the moment and thoroughly enraptured by my surroundings. I didn't have time to worry about the details. As Aliza had said, I was in Mexico. I just had to go with it!

CHAPTER TWENTY-TWO

PUMPKIN SEEDS

I believe empathy is the most essential quality of civilization.
—ROBERT EBERT

"Mom, do you think she earns five dollars a day?" Quinn asked stopping on the narrow sidewalk outside of the *Mercado 20 de Noviembre*.

The sun was low in the sky, casting long shadows across the cobblestone streets. Stalls lined the curb, selling everything from dried grasshoppers to plastic Tupperware, from socks and underwear to cell phone cases. People were weaving between the stalls and the street. The entrance to the market was flanked by women of all ages sitting on the sidewalk, their backs resting against the wall, baskets between their legs, trying to sell the last of their tamales, tortillas, and *tejate* drinks before darkness set in and the crowds of people headed home.

I loved *20 de Noviembre* and the area surrounding it. It was located just beyond the Santo Domingo Cathedral, the main tourist area. The *mercado*'s neighborhood wasn't as shiny or as polished. The streets were crowded. It was noisy. Street vendors yelled, taxis honked their horns, motorbikes whizzed through the intersections, and music played loudly. There was a mixture of smells: fresh flowers coupled with rotting vegetables that had fallen into the street, chicken roasting over an open fire mixed with the slightly rancid smell of raw pork and beef products covered with drab dish towels that were only marginally keeping the heat and flies at bay. This was where the locals lived, worked, and shopped. It felt gritty and real. I felt at home here. The neighborhood reminded me of living in Baltimore, and the *mercado* reminded me of Baltimore's Cross Street Market where I spent many weekends shopping for fruits and vegetables, bartering with the fishmongers, eating local foods, and maybe having a beer or two.

Quinn and I were running errands. We needed lemons. You can find limes everywhere in Oaxaca, but yellow lemons were sold at a few places and *20 de Noviembre* is one of them. We also needed to print a photo and a new strainer for the kitchen sink. A small photography stall was at the edge of the market, and a vendor sold strainers exclusively across the street. We bought mole paste and a chicken for dinner—*sin la cabeza pero con los pies* (without the head but with the feet). I am telling you, you can get everything you need at *20 de Noviembre!*

As we exited the market and headed back toward our car, I remembered Bill was planning to have some of his mountain biking amigos over for a post-ride beer and snack that evening. I had no snacks. I thought about re-entering the *mercado* to find veggies and *chicharrones* but didn't have it in me to navigate the labyrinth of stalls again to find what we were looking for.

That's when I saw her. An older woman with a basketful of roasted pumpkin seeds. That would work. She was tiny, wore a beautifully embroidered blouse and a full skirt, and her basket overflowed with pumpkin seeds in sandwich baggies. She was sitting on the sidewalk and stood as we approached her.

"How much for two bags?" I asked in my best Spanish.

"*Treinta pesos*," she responded, already reaching into the basket to pull out the bags of pumpkin seeds. Thirty pesos is roughly $1.50. I reached into my purse and pulled out a one hundred peso note, equivalent to five US dollars. I held the money out for her, but she would not take it. She looked from the note to me, shaking her head.

"*No tengo cambio* (I do not have change)," she said, her voice somewhat quiet among the competing noises of the street.

I smiled behind my COVID face covering to reassure her. I began looking for smaller bills or change in my purse. I found thirty pesos in loose change and held it up triumphantly.

"*Gracias a Dios*," she said offering thanks to God as she blessed herself with the sign of the cross. She accepted the change and deposited it into a small pouch that hung around her neck.

"*Muchas gracias*," I said as I took the bags and wished her a good evening.

A few yards down the street, Quinn asked about the five dollars. You see, a few days earlier, we'd been discussing a lesson Emily and Zane were studying in their world history class. It had become our renewed habit to talk about school and the impact of the lessons over dinner, a welcome change from our pre-Oaxaca discussions, which were all about logistics. That night's dinner discussion had been about the poverty line in the United States and around the world.

"Did you know almost 10 percent of the world's population lives on about two dollars per day?" Zane asked, grabbing a second helping of dinner.

"The difference between the rich and poor is crazy. Fewer than 10 percent of the world's population has almost all the money. What do they do with all of it?" Emily chimed in while passing the bowl of pasta across the table.

I loved this dinner discussion. It was deep and meaty. The kids were engaged. They were asking good questions, and I could almost see their brains expanding as they made connections in what they were learning. Sometimes I was still at a loss on how to respond to their questions. I often didn't have any answers, just more questions. One of those questions was "what was the poverty line in Mexico?"

For me, being so invested in what the kids were learning was incredible, because before Mexico, although I wouldn't say I was absent, I wasn't present either. Don't get me wrong; I cared about the kids' education. Of course I did. But our dinner conversations generally centered around "how was your day?" and "can you share one thing you learned?" to which the responses were usually "fine" or "I don't know." At some point, we instituted a rule no one could answer the highlight of their day was lunch or PE class. Once we got the perfunctory questions out of the way, we moved on to logistics: who was going where and what needed to get done the following day.

If you were to have looked at the division of parental labor between Bill and me, before my adult gap year, you would have found a relatively fair split. I was responsible for the doctor and dentist appointments, sports teams and camp sign-up, cooking, birthday parties, sending in stuff for class events, making sure shoes and clothes fit, maintaining the weekly calendar of events, and soccer carpools, among other things. Bill was responsible for laundry, coaching sports teams, breakfast and morning duty, bus stop drop-off, and all things school related. Bill loved it and was good at it. His favorite weekday break from work was to pop by the elementary school to volunteer in the classroom and grab lunch in the cafeteria with the kids. To me, that sounded like a migraine waiting to happen. Fortunately, or so I thought, meetings and clients kept me out of the school.

In Mexico, I had a deeper connection with the kids and knew what was going on in their education and day-to-day lives. School started at 6:30 a.m. for Emily and Zane. I would sit in Zane's room and *participate* in his first class of the day, physical education—my favorite was when the class did the *Just Dance* videos as their exercise. I loved listening to his teacher's gruff voice take attendance, the poor man repeating kids' names over and over again, trying to get them off mute. *Bueller, Bueller?* (Hughes 1986, 0:06:03–0:06:12).

Every other day, I sat in on Emily and Zane's Spanish class with their teacher, a quintessentially quirky middle school teacher who would dance and speak Spanish to her dogs. I joined Quinn for her morning meeting almost every day. I learned about her classmates, what they liked and what they wanted to be that day, as it was ever-changing (Maya wanted to be a big cat trainer, and Joe was getting a new dog). I knew what Quinn's class was working on. I was invested. I was watching them learn, grow, and become new people before my eyes. I had never experienced this before, and I loved it.

Quinn had asked the question about the Mexican poverty line during our dinner conversation. We had to look it up on Google. According to the World Bank, over 40 percent of Mexico's population falls below the national poverty line, living on the equivalent of approximately five US dollars per day (World Bank 2020). Poverty levels are even higher in the southern states of Mexico. In Oaxaca, approximately 66 percent of the population lives in poverty (Shvili 2021).

So when Quinn asked if the woman earned five dollars a day, I had an idea of where she was going with this. "I don't know," I said. "What do you think?" Although Quinn was only nine, she was logical, thoughtful, and empathetic. Some have said she has an old soul.

"Well, it's getting late. It's like 4:30 p.m., and her basket is still full. She didn't have change for one hundred pesos. That's not a lot of money." Quinn looked back at the woman, who had bent down to rearrange her basket. "So no, I don't think she makes five dollars a day."

I looked at my logical and empathetic daughter. She looked wounded by the thought this person, whom we had just conversed with was working hard to sell her goods but made so little money. I brushed her hair, tucked it behind her ear, and said, "No, I don't think so either, baby."

Quinn kicked at a loose sidewalk brick, looked up at me, and asked, "Mom, can I have those one hundred pesos? I will pay you back when we get home?"

I handed her the money without hesitation. Sure, I could have told Quinn she should buy more pumpkin seeds from the woman, or we could donate to a charity that might make a bigger impact on the poverty that affects so many across Oaxaca, but this was Quinn's act of kindness. This was the way her nine-year-old brain was seeing a problem, processing information, and taking action. Her way of connecting to our family's value of "building others up with our actions and our words." I watched as Quinn ran back to the woman who had sold us our snacks. Quinn engaged in a brief conversation with her as she offered her the money. The woman graciously accepted the pesos and offered thanks to my daughter.

Quinn turned and skipped back to me. She removed her mask and was smiling. "What did you say to her?" I asked because Quinn was not overly confident in speaking in Spanish.

"I told her I wanted her to have the money. That I thought her skirt was really pretty. And I wished her a good day. At least I hope I did. I was really nervous." I squeezed Quinn's hand, and we walked toward our car.

I was proud of Quinn. It wasn't as if this was the first time she had helped someone less fortunate than her. She had volunteered in our community, at school, and with the Girl Scouts. But something was different, distant perhaps, about volunteering in Virginia. These were activities she'd participated in as part of a larger group, where she was assigned a task. This day her act of kindness had been of her own volition. I was proud she had processed information, connected dots, overcome her fears of speaking Spanish, and reached out to another person.

As I reflected on our afternoon later that evening, I knew in my heart we could have talked to our kids until we were blue in the face about income inequality and true abject poverty. I know it existed all around us, even at home, but sometimes it was harder to see, or perhaps sadly, it was easier to ignore. In Oaxaca, it was everywhere. We were forced to confront people who were not on the margins but were the majority. We interacted with these people, bought food from them, invited them into our home to work for us, looked them in the eye, and talked with them. Poverty is more than just a concept; it is a reality Oaxaca, Mexico, and the rest of the world struggle with.

I questioned the fairness and impact of my decision on my family many times throughout my adult gap year. At that moment I knew, however, Bill and I had given our kids and ourselves the gift of expanding our world and viewpoint beyond northern Virginia, while bringing the people who live in it a little bit closer to us and into our hearts.

CHAPTER TWENTY-THREE

WHAT'S YOUR PLAN?

Life isn't about finding yourself.
Life is about creating yourself.
—GEORGE BERNARD SHAW

"What is your plan for your adult gap year?" Bill asked as he walked through the kitchen on his way to his office. He had no malice in his question, no hidden agenda. He was genuinely curious. For me, however, the question landed with the force of a boulder, heavy upon my chest. I couldn't breathe. The truth was, when I started my adult gap year, I had no idea what I was doing. For once in my life, I had no plan.

Assuming I could work my way into an answer, I typed, "What to do during an adult gap year?" into Google. The results were limited. Most sites targeted younger people taking a gap year before or after college and included objectives like pursuing your passion, traveling the world, immersing yourself in a new culture, volunteering, or exploring a new career path. These were good but not a plan or a checklist.

I wanted something that said, "You are here," followed by step one, step two, and so on. Since that didn't exist, I cobbled one together on my own.

YOU ARE HERE: OAXACA.
I've always been a runner. I've run marathons. I've run the kids from one activity to another. I've approached my career like an all-out sprint, running as fast as I could, hellbent on getting somewhere, anywhere as quickly as possible.

You're like Scooby-Doo. I see your legs moving, but you ain't getting anywhere!

It wasn't sustainable. Not for me. Not for my family.

But where do you go from here?

"I should be able to figure this out," I said a week into my adult gap year. Bill was floating in the pool, while I paced alongside. My frustration manifested itself into a brisk walk.

"*Should* is a dangerous word," said Bill. "Really, you *get to* figure it out. You can decide what you want your life to be. That's an opportunity."

Should. Get to. What's the difference? I was trying to be upbeat. But undertaking a process where you're effectively dismantling your life, challenging your assumptions, questioning your decisions, and rebuilding something hopefully better is scary in the beginning. Being someone who works with speed and efficiency, I wanted to blow through this to get to the other side—whatever the other side may be. But I didn't have a clue where to start and that was unnerving.

As if reading my mind, Bill said, "You've never done this before. Cut yourself some slack." With that, he dove underwater and started swimming his laps.

STEP ONE: SLOW DOWN.
On the surface, slowing down seemed easy enough. Sit in a chair. Read a book. Don't check your email every three minutes. Do nothing. How hard can that be?

In reality, it was anything but easy. I had been sprinting for so long stopping felt unnatural, and jarring, like when you hit the emergency stop on a treadmill. When I stopped doing, I found I was fighting myself and the patterns that had made me successful all my life.

During the day, I was anxious and frustrated. *You're not doing enough. You're being lazy. If you want to solve this problem, you need to work harder.* I tried to shake the voices of my internal shitty committee.

During the night, panic would wake me. *Where am I? What did I forget to do?* I clutched my chest and tried to catch my breath. "You're on sabbatical. Relax; you have nothing to worry about," I'd reassure myself in a whisper. My heart rate would begin to slow. And I thought, *This is never going to work. You are meant to charge hard; it's who you are.*

I wanted to move forward to a new way of being, but my muscle memory kept holding onto old habits. "It's like you're a pressure cooker," a friend said over a Zoom happy hour. She had a glass of wine, and I had a glass of mezcal. "You've been removed from the flame, but the steam hasn't been released yet. And unfortunately, there's no quick release for the pressure you've built up."

Shit. She's right. Slowing down was going to take longer than I want it to.

STEP TWO: BE PRESENT.
I heard enough about the benefits of mindfulness I figured I'd give it a try. *Be present. Be in the moment. Enjoy what you're doing.*

Unfortunately, being present also proved difficult. Because even when I was able to stop moving and slow down, thoughts about work, life in the US, and my big question of what I was going to do next were still there. These thoughts crept in all the time; they were ever present. It felt like the continued presence of my worries was the only presence I could find.

Why is it so hard to be present?

It's not just me who struggles with presence. It's all humans. It's how we're wired to survive. Most other species survive using their instincts and reactions (Winter 2016). Their fight-or-flight mechanisms rule the day. Humans, on the other hand, reflect on the past, learn from that past, and plan for the future. It's how we've adapted, evolved, and flourished. It is, however, what makes being in the present so difficult. The present is but a fleeting moment, here and gone. The present becomes the past, over which we can ruminate.

Jon Kabat-Zinn, author of *Wherever You Go, There You Are*, defines mindfulness as "paying attention in a particular way: on purpose, in the present moment, and non-judgmentally" (Kabat-Zinn 1994). This was the type of mindfulness I was experiencing. Everything was new—the language I was learning, the hills I was walking, the streets I was exploring, the life I was creating. I was forced to pay attention. I couldn't operate on autopilot.

I appreciated where I was and what I was accomplishing. Even the littlest things—like hearing the difference between sixty—*sesenta*—and seventy—*setenta*—or calling the water company and actually having them arrive with jugs of drinking water. These were huge accomplishments. I was there for every moment. This was mindfulness.

Soon my ability to be present transcended beyond exploring my environment. When I thought of the past, it was not about "work Suzanne." Rather, I thought about things I did when I was younger, activities I would like to try again—painting, cooking, and reading for fun. When I spent time with my family, I was really with them. I listened to their thoughts, feelings, and concerns. I got to know them on a deeper level. Ours was a shared experience. All of us were changing in ways that were hard to measure at the moment. The present had become a gift.

STEP THREE: MOVE FORWARD.
Move. Put one foot in front of the other. Right foot. Left foot. It doesn't matter how fast you go. It only matters you are moving forward. I needed to make progress so walking became my thing. It was simple. It was active. If I was moving, I was making progress. Having an achievable goal was comforting.

I walked to the local *mercado* to go shopping and wandered through the aisles of stalls. Colors popped from the fruit and vegetable displays. Chilis in every color, deep red strawberries, golden pineapples—everything seemed more vibrant here—it reminded me of when Dorothy got to Oz. The air was filled with unfamiliar smells—*herba santos, epazote,* and *chapulines* (dried crickets)—that were rich, earthy, and intriguing. I lingered among the stalls to practice my Spanish listening skills. When I was in the market, I wasn't in a hurry.

I walked Tilly on the nearby mountain trails, up the steep hills, and through fields dotted with silver-blue agave plants. I stopped to talk with farmers heading out to their fields. I practiced my hello in my head so I could confidently greet people. "*Buen día. Es un día hermoso para caminar con mi perro. Que tengas un buen día* (Good morning. It's a beautiful day to walk with my dog. I hope you have a good day)." This way, if I accidentally wandered onto someone's property, they would let me pass through.

Eventually, my walks became more of a moving meditation rather than merely a form of transportation. I left my AirPods behind, walking without music, audiobooks, or podcasts. I began to notice my mind was less cluttered, which allowed me to take in my surroundings. The more I walked, the more I found myself stopping. Stopping to listen. Stopping to talk. Stopping to appreciate where I was. Oddly, it was by moving forward I finally found a way to slow down and be fully present.

STEP FOUR: LET GO OF EXPECTATIONS.
"What do you want your life to look like?" Rodrigo, my coach, asked me across the Zoom video conference. He was in his home office in Mexico City; I was on spring break with my family in the lake town of Valle de Bravo.

I don't know. Simple, I guess. I have no idea what that looks like, though.

"I guess I want a life that feels like my Birkenstocks," I said, looking away from my computer screen and across to the lake. I was searching for words to explain what I wanted. All I could think of was a shoe another metaphor. "I brought high heels with me to Oaxaca. I thought we might get invited to a party. I wanted to be able to fit in, to play the part if I had to. But once we got here, I realized heels are completely impractical."

In Oaxaca, I don't have to live up to anyone else's expectations. I don't know anyone. I had no one to disappoint. It's been nice. I'm so tired of playing a part.

"I always wanted Birkenstocks, but I've got big feet. I thought other people would think I looked stupid—like Fred Flintstone or something. I never allowed myself to buy a pair."

I don't want to be judged, at least not in a negative way. I am afraid of looking stupid. I put intense pressure on myself to be the best, to work the hardest, to be successful, and to be seen as perfect. I don't want to let myself or anyone else down. But it's a performance. And I'm exhausted.

"I bought a pair of Birkenstocks when we got to Mexico, and I've discovered they're not only practical but they're comfortable too. My Birkenstocks are molded to my feet."

I can be myself here. When I meet people, they get all of me. Even the parts that are searching and growing. I'm not trying to play a part. They liked me for me. I'm enough without my title and my stuff. When I butcher their language and make faux pas after faux pas, I am enough. I never believed that before. I need to let go of my fear people will judge me and I will disappoint them. And I need to let go of the expectations and pressure I put on myself. Frankly, I need to be nicer to me.

"So yeah. I guess I want my life to look like my Birkenstocks. Something simple and practical, but something that is molded to me. Not a life where I mold myself into a version of me others want."

STEP FIVE: ACCEPT FEEDBACK.

"I don't want you to go back to work," said Quinn as we gathered around the dinner table, talking about what it might be like when we returned to Virginia. "You're better as *Oaxaca mom*. Better than when you were *work mom*. Can you please be *Oaxaca mom* all the time, even when we're not in Oaxaca?"

This one hurt. Quinn's comment was like a knife to my heart, a knife that had been twisted for good measure. Part of me rationalized I worked so hard so I could show my children what being a strong, successful woman could look like. I operated under the impression my kids were proud of me because of my successful career. *Maybe I was wrong.* Or maybe Quinn was just more right. It's not she didn't care about my achievements. She understood what was important and she was proud of me no matter what. Quinn saw a better way for me to be.

We are not systems unto ourselves. Every day we make choices that impact those around us. I didn't like Quinn's feedback. She'd held up a mirror for me to see myself, and I saw the choices I made to achieve my so-called successes were hurting others. I wasn't as good as I thought I was. Once I heard Quinn's feedback, I had a choice to make. I could go back to my old habits where work was my priority and my family (even though it was really hard to admit) came second, where I would squeeze them in if I could and put work commitments ahead of their needs almost like their needs were optional. Or, I could honor myself and the people I valued most, by making all of us my main priority.

The decision was clear. No one wants to be an option.

STEP SIX: PICK UP THE PUZZLE PIECES.
Signs are everywhere if you choose to see them.

It's not I didn't believe in signs; I just never took the time to look for them. I moved fast, racing through my five- and ten-year plans. If an opportunity appeared that wasn't part of the plan, the door had better open and knock me over so I could see it.

When I made space for silence and presence and when I understood myself better, I could see pieces to the puzzle of my life I would have missed before.

I want to use my unique skills.

I'd been trying to figure out other potential career paths, and I was stuck. I barged into the living room where Bill and the kids were cuddled up watching a movie. Armed with a stack of sticky notes and markers, I practically begged for their help. "You guys know me. What am I good at? What should I be doing?"

My family came through. In fewer than ten minutes they had stacks of ideas where they thought I excelled and possible careers that might be a fit.

- Staying focused
- Project management
- Going outside of your comfort zone
- A camp director, a bartender, a therapist
- A creative, an artist, a designer, a storyteller
- A chef
- Making people happy
- A teacher (but not for little kids; you're not really good with little kids)
- A butler

"A butler, Quinn? Really?" I asked as visions of an old British man dressed in a tux popped into my head.

"Hold on. Hear me out; you're good at organizing things, and you're really good at spending other people's money," Quinn said, with a giggle and a mischievous look.

Well, she had a point.

Their ideas were creative and thoughtful. They saw strengths in me I didn't always see in myself. And although a career didn't jump out at me and I didn't know what I would do with the list, I liked it. I saved it. It was a puzzle piece I might need later.

I want to help people.

I applied as a volunteer story writer for Fundación En Vía, an organization that provides microfinance loans to women in the indigenous communities surrounding Oaxaca. I wanted to capture the stories of the indigenous women who received these twenty-five-dollar loans to launch a business. But En Vía wanted me to design their post-pandemic operating strategy. It wasn't the role I wanted. It seemed too close to "work Suzanne." I was nervous I would fall back to my old ways. I said yes anyway.

Designing and facilitating En Vía's two-day strategy session was one of the most difficult things I'd ever done. And one of the most rewarding. I conducted the session entirely in Spanish. Even though I knew little about these women's lives, I made a positive impact. I was curious and listened. I asked questions and created space for their creativity to shine through.

Over the two days, the women transform from timid and quiet to confident and outspoken. They were the experts in their lives, not me. They knew what they wanted and needed: more chickens to grow their egg production businesses, support for online marketing, and enhanced microfinance loan structures.

I transformed too, from a person who excelled because she had all the answers, to someone who could lead from behind and still make a positive impact. From someone who had been apathetic about their work to someone who was consumed with the passion of helping people.

I want to connect the dots.

My inner voice had been loud and clear on my silent yoga retreat. *I want to design.* It surprised me. I didn't know what I was supposed to do with the message at the time.

I simply filed it away for later. And one day a few months later, I was listening to a podcast when I heard a Chief Design Officer say, "Design is not this aesthetic exercise. Design is about helping people make sense of the world" (Giudice 2016).

Boom! This was the puzzle piece that made my *I want to design* epiphany come into focus. It was the puzzle piece I'd been looking for. Helping people make sense of their world—I did that all the time. I was already a designer.

I collected puzzle pieces throughout my adult gap year. Sometimes the picture was clear, and I knew exactly what to do with this new piece of the puzzle. Other times, I had a distinct feeling the piece could change the ultimate picture. But that was the fun part. I used to know where I was going, but I could barely enjoy the ride. This time, I wasn't sure where I was going, but I was having fun picking up the pieces along the way and figuring out the picture in the puzzle.

When I put the pieces together, I saw it: For me, it's all about people. They are at the heart of every complex problem. At my core, I create connections, spark creativity, and facilitate experiences to help others unlock their full potential.

STEP SEVEN: REFLECT.
My adult gap year never really translated into a formal plan where I could check things off my list. Rather, it evolved like a flower opening to reveal something

unexpected, yet beautiful. I simply kept doing the next thing: making the next call to get things done at the house, reading the next book because I was interested in the topic, and taking the next class. Whether art, cooking, or leadership design I was picking up the next puzzle piece. I kept moving forward. I learned new things. I sought feedback. I iterated, incorporated my learnings, and started again.

When Bill asked about my adult gap year, I thought I needed a plan. But I didn't. I needed to work the process. I needed to unlearn and relearn. In the end, my adult gap year taught me:

- There is value in slowing down.
- Freedom in letting go.
- I am a hell of a lot stronger than I ever gave myself credit for.
- When I listened to my heart and the universe, I found my way forward.

In the end, I am living my life to the best of my ability, loving fiercely, living fully, taking risks, learning more, and trusting myself. Because I'm supposed to be doing this.

CHAPTER TWENTY-FOUR

BITTERSWEET

*"O divine chocolate, we grind it on our knees,
we beat it with our hands in prayer and we drink it
with our eyes lifted to the heavens."*
—ANCIENT MEXICAN SAYING

I was dreading this trip—my last trip to Centro on my own. My last day to explore the streets unencumbered by time or task. On days like this, in Centro by myself, I adopted a state of what the French call *flâner*, wandering the streets with no destination in mind. I would turn right or left as the whim hit me. I would duck down alleyways or through doorways into intriguing courtyards shaded from the heat. My goal was one of exploration and "to be at once part of a place and to be on the outside, observing" (Monaco 2019).

Today I wanted to take it all in, to remember it all. It was mid-May, the sun was high overhead, the sky was a crystal *azul*, and white cumulus clouds dotted the horizon. I felt little relief from the heat. I walked slowly down Calle de Reforma. The two-story colonial buildings on either side of the street were painted in shades of salmon, blues, and yellows. The street was dirt strewn, but as the heat rose from it in wisps, the cobblestones shimmered a silvery glow. Mexican *banda* music drifted into the street from the window of a café, and the smell of roasting cacao beans permeated the air.

As I rounded the corner the line for *Chocolate Mayordomo* stretched out ahead of me. *Mayordomo* is considered to be Oaxaca's best chocolatier, and the line to enter the building supported that statement. Some of the people waiting online were holding large buckets, filled with their family's recipe of cacao beans, sugar, cinnamon, and almonds, waiting for the mixture to be ground into chocolate in the large electric grinders. Others were waiting to buy *Mayordomo*'s pre-made chocolate mixture. Still, others were waiting to enjoy an afternoon treat of hot chocolate and thick egg bread. The red and white awning flapped in the breeze and beckoned me with the promise of shade, along with a few boxes of chocolate to take home as gifts. I jumped into my place in line.

The line inched forward. No one was in a rush, nor was I. After eight months, we were going home to Virginia in a few days. It seemed our Oaxacan adventure was coming to an end in a flash, and yet in other more profound ways it felt like we had left the US a lifetime ago.

We'd grown as a family and as individuals. We navigated the unknown—often fumbling our way through customs and culture, but for the most part, making it out on top. We leaned into each other—for companionship, for familiarity, for figuring out how to do the most mundane tasks on a day-to-day basis. Our family bond was stronger than ever. We'd taken risks—riding mountain biking, learning a language, deepening our artistic skills, riding horses—and despite bumps and bruises (some literal and others just to our ego), we bounced back time and time again. We reached out, made connections, and forged friendships—on the golf course, in the classroom, on the basketball court, at a yoga retreat, on horseback, in the countryside, and on the hiking and biking trails. Our world is equally bigger and smaller because of these connections. We left behind the life we'd known and created a new life for ourselves in Oaxaca.

And my growth—I was not the same person I was when I left Virginia. No longer consumed by stress and worry. No longer driven by the need to accumulate more or to be recognized for what I did. My goal in coming to Oaxaca was to do better for myself and for my family. Because I knew I could do better, I had to do better. And I was better—not perfect, but better. I learned to slow down so I could reconnect with who I was and who I wanted to be. I found a way to prioritize what is important to me and a way to stay true to my values. I discovered a path forward where I could impact people in a positive and transformative way. Where I could help them to become better leaders and to lead richer lives. Where I would help them to unlock their full potential.

As I moved toward *Mayordomo*, I took in my surroundings. The colors were so vibrant they were almost infectious. The brightness reached into my soul and buoyed me. The smells—chocolate mixed with the ever-present and underlying smell of sulfur. *I will miss this.* The people—bustling here and there, but willing to lend a hand. The food—fresh and spicy. *Please let me remember how to make tamales.* The sounds—the ever-present horn that sounded like a cow mooing and the jingle of the *Gas de Oaxaca* truck. *Would I be able to find the jingle to use as an alarm?* I smiled at the thought.

I gained so much in Oaxaca, and for that I was thankful, but I would miss so much. Wandering the streets, speaking Spanish, and pushing myself every day. The duality of a life that was complicated yet simple at the same time. I didn't want to leave. I felt rooted in place because I had put down roots in Oaxaca. These roots would stay connected to this earth. Hopefully, I could stay connected to the version of me I discovered here.

"*Pardon, señora,*" said the man behind the counter, interrupting my thoughts. The line had moved forward. It was time for me to move too. "*Chocolate dulce o chocolate medio* (Sweet chocolate or bittersweet chocolate)?"

I hiccupped an answer through my emotions. "*Chocolate medio, por favor.* (Bittersweet, please)."

"The bittersweet side of appreciating life's most precious moment is the unbearable awareness that those moments are passing" (Parent 2002). Like the chocolate, this moment, this time was bittersweet. It was time to go home. I longed for my dishwasher, to hug my family, and to see our friends. My adult gap year was technically over.

I would miss Oaxaca, but I wasn't leaving, not really. I was leaving a bit of my heart there and taking so much more with me. I placed my chocolate in my bag and headed back to the car park, lost in my thoughts and memories. As I drove toward the foothills and our house, I passed the Zocalo, Santo Domingo, and Llano Park; the women selling pumpkin seeds and tamales; the jugglers in the intersection; women on buses headed to destinations unknown; and men wheeling their taco stands to Centro. All these sights were part of our home now, part of me.

I glanced in my rearview mirror as the sights of Centro faded and whispered, "*Hasta luego, Oaxaca. Mi amor.*"

EPILOGUE

Travel changes you. As you move through this life and this world you change things slightly, you leave marks behind, however small. And in return, life—and travel— leaves marks on you.
—ANTHONY BOURDAIN

It's been two years since I listened to my internal voice that urged me I could do better, and once again, we were boarding a plane to Oaxaca. Not to move this time—we were merely heading back for a two-week vacation to cement memories, reconnect with friends, and celebrate all that has changed since I first uttered the words, "What if we moved to Mexico?"

A lot had changed since that day. I describe my re-entry into our US lives like putting on a shoe that had been an old favorite (go figure—another show metaphor). Everything about the shoe looked familiar and should be comfortable, but when I tried it on, it was a little too tight. Everything felt a bit smaller in Virginia. We had grown and changed, and it felt a bit awkward to return to normal. But we did.

We fell back into rhythms and routines without too much prompting. We met friends, saw family, and rejoined sports teams. I returned to my role as a partner in my management consulting firm, albeit in a more people-focused practice. I even succumbed to the allure of online shopping—although I was more selective in what I bought. The gravitational pull of our *before life* was strong. We were busy again.

But even in the busy, I see the impact of Oaxaca shining through. My family is collectively pushing back on gravity by holding onto whom we became in Mexico.

For Emily, whose desire to come home was the strongest, it shows up in her commitment to developing her Spanish language skills. After the first week of high school, Emily came home from school and announced, "It's funny, but now I am home, I see what a great experience we had. I want to take the test to see if I qualify for the fluent Spanish class. I really want to be able to study abroad to see and experience more of the world."

For Zane, it is in his desire to help others. "I realize how blessed and fortunate we are. In Mexico, we met people who would go out of their way to help others. When we were biking, we'd stop to help strangers repair their bikes and sometimes even their cars. It didn't matter. People needed help so we would help them. During my bike race here the other day, a guy wrecked close to the finish. Most people passed him. I thought of the bike group in Oaxaca. I stopped."

For Quinn, it shows up in almost everything she does. Maybe it is because our time in Oaxaca represents almost a quarter of her active memories since she was four. She is my traditions kid. Quinn reminds us to celebrate the holidays of Mexico. She sets up our altar for Día de Los Muertos, makes piñatas for Christmas, helps me make the tamales, and she makes sure we see and help our neighbors who are less fortunate than we are.

For Bill, it shows up in his appreciation. He is thankful for what we have, even more so than before, that we were able to give our family this opportunity, and for the friendships we made. Bill went out of his way to make friends with local *Oaxacaqueños*, and he takes time to nurture these friendships and our connection to our second home.

For me, the journey didn't end when I stepped through the door to my house, dropping my stuff on the mudroom floor. I continue to learn and push myself. Expanding my skills and exploring how I can intentionally live my life. I take classes, read books, practice being present, and lean into my core strengths. I am committed to not wasting my Adult Gap Year. Every day I attempt to practice what I learned in Oaxaca because I am a work in progress.

On July 31, 2022, I stepped away from my role as a partner at the management consulting firm, where I had been for almost twenty-two years, to launch my own business: Vamonos Executive Coaching. My decision to leave wasn't entered lightly. But I knew, from the work I had done, I wasn't running away from something but running toward something new, exciting, and energizing. Something I was called to do.

Am I better than I was in 2020? I don't know. I'd like to think so. But I am living my life in a way that aligns with my purpose and values. I am open to opportunities; my decisions are intentional; I'm not afraid to make a mistake; and I am not constantly looking for approval from others. For this I am grateful. And when I need to slow down, I know where I am headed—back to Oaxaca to reconnect with me. Every day our full potential awaits. *Vamonos... Let's go!*

ACKNOWLEDGMENTS

I am grateful for all the people who supported me on my journey to figure out what I'm supposed to be doing and encouraged me to tell my story.

To Oaxaca and our friends there, *gracias por recibirnos en tu casa y compartir tu magia con nosotros. Cambiaste mi vida para mejor.* Chris and Miriam, for the hours you spent teaching us Spanish and being our friends. The Abdiases, for sharing your home and Gatito with us; she is forever our cat. Federico and Patricia Sada, and Hugo and Pau Felix, for taking a chance on the gringos; your friendship means the world. Mary Jane Gagnier, for taking Quinn under your wing and introducing her to her passion for horse riding. Marlin, and Next Level Oaxaca, for welcoming Emily and Zane onto the basketball team and showing them teamwork and laughter overcomes language barriers. LeAnn and Marty, for showing us what is possible and for the tacos—lots and lots of tacos. Ellen, for walking the hills with me. And to everyone else whom I missed but played a part in making our experience in Oaxaca so wonderful, *muchas gracias. Un pedazo de mi corazón siempre estará contigo.*

To my colleagues and friends who supported me when I stepped away from the firm, who made sure I took advantage of the opportunity, and who encouraged me to follow my passion of launching my own business, thank you. To all the pink unicorns who dare to dream we can work differently, don't give up. The unicorn preserve will exist, and you will change the way work gets done. To the leaders who inspired me, who thought differently and lead authentically, for challenging me and guiding me to discover my passion—you saw potential in me beyond what I even knew was possible at the time. I grew up in the firm, and it made me who I am. To my partners and team members, thank you for your friendship, for the laughter, for the late nights, for my personal and intellectual growth, and for allowing me to be part of a wonderful group of professionals. You are what I miss most.

To the Husdon Coaching Institute HCC fall 2021 cohort, my SLG (Stephanie, Natalie, Rob, Michelle, Andrea, Christie, and Carrie), LifeForward group (Robby, Sanobar, David, Marie, Jeff, Michelle, and Janaki), and my mentor coaches (Tom, Seth, Keith, Joy, Aiko, Toni, Pam, and Michael), thank you for showing me I have nowhere to go and only growing to do.

To my author's community: Your support turned my pages into the reality of this book. You came together from so many paths of my life I have walked—friends and family from my childhood to today, from elementary school to college, from the neighborhood to my professional world. Thank you, Kate and Matt Ahrens, Yasi Akbari, Chuck Ament, Charles Baird, Tamara Baker,

Koert Bakker, Michelle Berberian, Varun Bhaskar, Mark Biancaniello, Paula and Joe Birkenstock, Jennie Blumenthal, Cathy Bonner, Sarah Bowman and Scott Fisher, Jean and EB Bowman, Randi Braun, Dr. Jennie Byrne, Tanya Carlson, James Chidichimo, Don Christian, Sharvari Chwastyk, Tara Claeys, Rachel Clark, Mary Jo and Jim Fisher, Andrea Florence, Dave Franklin, Melanie and Rick Frick, Kate Frost, Bob Gallagher, David Gonzalez, Steven Gragg, Michael Green, Teresa Green, Cliff Greenblatt, Kate Hawkens, Coleen Howard, Jeff Jaworski, Avery Joshua, Carrie Kenney-McWilliams, Molly and John Ketcham, Karin Kirchoff, Eric Koester, Gayle Lang, Samantha Lanier, Jamie Larsen, Stacy Leff, Jen Lewi, Swati Limaye, Denise and Anthony Lucadamo, Meredith Mark, LeAnn and Marty Mastera, Connell McConeghy, Traci McDonald, Holly McKenzie, Sanobar Mehta, Paul Mihalick, Kim and Chuck Miller, Amber Moody, Jessica Morris, Meredith Murphy, Christie Myers, Jennifer and Todd Nash, Kareem Neal, Jamie Norris, Melissa and Don O'Neill, Shawn O'Hara and Steve Binder, Wally Okpych, Karyn Patino, Ellen Perkins, Matt Popham, Lisa Powers, Laura Preng and Tony Frank, George Prokop, Lori and Joey Reale, Kimberly Manno Reott, Tom Reott, Tyler and Julie Rinker, Cheryl Riporti, Heather Rosenberg-Hirshfield, Julie Sherman, David and Heather Sieradski, Michelle Sirott, Cheryl Sjolseth, Stacie and Stuart Sperry, Marie Szuts, Kristin Torcasi, Sara Verdugo, Rachel and Brian Walsh, Kristen and Andy Weetenkamp, Ellen and Eric Witter, Deb Wituski and Greg Strizek, Susan Wright, Koutayba Yasmak, and Helena Yoon. I am truly humbled by your support.

To my writing and editing team at the Creators Institute and New Degree Press, including Eric Koester, my developmental editor Scott Aronowitz, my revisions editor Kari Wolfe, my wrangler Jacques Moolman—thank you for your encouragement, input, and patience. Scott, I may finally understand the point of an introduction. To my beta readers team, Deb, Paul, Marie, Laura, and Meredith, for your constructive and thoughtful critiques.

To all my friends who supported me/us throughout this journey—David, Heather, Deb, and Greg—for encouraging us to go, even if you really wanted us to stay, and for watching the house while we were in Mexico. Sanjay and Holly for encouraging me to run toward what I wanted, even if it was unconventional. Randi for pushing me to share my story, introducing me to the Creators Institute, and reminding me my heart knows the way. Paul for the catchphrase, "I'm supposed to be doing this." Who knew it would come in so handy? You should have trademarked it. And to my team who always have my back—Kimberly, Melanie, Kristen, Rosie, Laura, Molly, Holly, Deb, Meredith, and so many others—thank you for your unwavering support. I love you.

To my parents, I lucked out when I got you. Thank you for teaching me the value of hard work and I can do anything I put my mind to. You have always been my biggest advocates. To Scott and Sarah, for always being there for all of us. And to Rosie—you taught me to be tough and to laugh at myself. You are all my village, and I wouldn't have had the courage to make these changes in my life without your support.

Finally, to my heart: Bill, Emily, Zane, and Quinn. This journey, both to Oaxaca and in life, would be meaningless without you. Thank you for your unwavering support and encouragement. I am grateful we were able to grow together as individuals and as a family. Always remember we are kind, smart, and tough. *Vamonos!*

APPENDIX

INTRODUCTION

Brown, Brené. 2020. *The Gifts of Imperfection: 10th Anniversary Edition.* New York, NY: Penguin Random House LLC.

Brown, Brené. 2018. "The Midlife Unraveling." *Articles Midlife* (blog), May 24, 2018. https://brenebrown.com/articles/2018/05/24/the-midlife-unraveling/.

Ewing-Nelson, Claire. 2021. *All of the Jobs Lost in December Were Women's Jobs.* Washington, DC: National Women's Law Center.

Gilbert, Elizabeth. 2006. *Eat, Pray, Love: One Woman's Search for Everything Across Italy, India and Indonesia.* New York, NY: Riverhead Books.

Horn, Michael B. 2020. "Unprecedented Numbers of Students Are Taking a Gap Year. What Should They Do with the Time?" *EdSurge.* August 17, 2020. https://www.edsurge.com/news/2020-08-17-unprecedented-numbers-of-students-are-taking-a-gap-year-what-should-they-do-with-the-time (accessed October 10, 2022).

Kellett, Ann. 2022. "The Texas A&M Professor Who Predicted 'The Great Resignation.'" *Texas A&M Today*. February 11, 2022. https://today.tamu.edu/2022/02/11/the-texas-am-professor-who-predicted-the-great-resignation/ (accessed October 4, 2022).

SHRM. 2022. "Interactive Chart: How Historic Has the Great Resignation Been?" SHRM Talent Acquisitions. October 2, 2022. https://www.shrm.org/resourcesandtools/hr-topics/talent-acquisition/pages/interactive-quits-level-by-year.aspx.

CHAPTER TWO

Winfrey, Oprah. 2014. *What I know for Sure*. New York, NY: Hearst Communications, Inc.

CHAPTER FOUR

Levine, Ken. *Bioshock*. Irrational Games. PC / XBox360. 2007.

CHAPTER SIX

Chekhov, Anton. 2015. *Ivanoff: A Play*. New York, NY: Yurita Press.

CHAPTER SEVEN

Lewis, C.S. 1960. *The Four Loves*. New York, NY: Harcourt, Brace.

CHAPTER EIGHT

Merriam-Webster Online Dictionary, s.v. 2021. *Merriam-Webster Online Dictionary*. Springfield, MA: Merriam-Webster, Inc. https://www.merriam-webster.com/dictionary/authentic.

Oxford Learner's Dictionaries, s.v. 2022. Oxford Learner's Dictionaries. Oxford, England: Oxford University Press. https://www.oxfordlearnersdictionaries.com/us/definition/english/golden-thread?q=golden+thread.

Winfrey, Oprah. 2010. "What Oprah Knows for Sure About Finding Your Calling." *O, The Oprah Magazine.* November 2010. https://www.oprah.com/spirit/oprah-on-finding-your-calling-what-i-know-for-sure (accessed October 11, 2022).

CHAPTER NINE

Barks, Coleman. 1995. *The Essential Rumi.* New York, NY: HarperCollins.

CHAPTER TEN

Doyle, Glennon. 2020. *Untamed.* New York, NY: The Dial Press.

CHAPTER ELEVEN

Parton, Dolly. 2012. *Dream More: Celebrate the Dreamer in You.* New York, NY: Riverhead Books.

CHAPTER THIRTEEN

Feiler, Bruce. 2013. *The Secrets of Happy Families: Improve Your Mornings, Tell Your Family History, Fight Smarter, Go Out and Play, and Much More.* New York, NY: William Morrow.

CHAPTER FOURTEEN

Estrem, Pauline. 2021. "Why Failure is Good for Success." *Success Marketing* (blog). August 11, 2021. https://www.success.com/why-failure-is-good-for-success/.

Hendry, Erica R. 2013. "7 Epic Fails Brought to You by the Genius Mind of Thomas Edison." *Smithsonian Magazine,* November 2013. https://www.smithsonianmag.com/innovation/7-epic-fails-brought-to-you-by-the-genius-mind-of-thomas-edison-180947786/ (accessed on October 15, 2022).

Merriam-Webster Online Dictionary, s.v. 2021. *Merriam-Webster Online Dictionary.* Springfield, MA: Merriam-Webster, Inc. https://www.merriam-webster.com/dictionary/failure.

CHAPTER FIFTEEN

Jung, C. G. 1933. *Modern Man in Search of a Soul.* Translation by W.S. Dell and Cary F. Baynes. New York, NY: A Harvest Book, Harcourt, Inc.

CHAPTER SEVENTEEN

Marca País. n.d. "Guelaguetza: Celebrating Oaxacan Culture." *Discover Oaxaca Festivals and Holidays* (blog). https://discover-oaxaca.com/festivals-and-holidays/guelaguet-

za-celebrating-oaxacan-culture/#:~:text=The%20word%20
Guelaguetza%20means%20%E2%80%9Coffering,a%20
reciprocal%20exchange%20between%20parties (accessed
October 17, 2022).

CHAPTER EIGHTEEN

Hudson, Frederic M. 1999. *The Adult Years: Mastering the Art of Self-Renewal*. San Francisco, CA: Jossey-Bass.

Hudson Institute. 2022. LifeForward. Hudson Institute. Accessed October 24, 2022. https://hudsoninstitute.com/individuals/lifeforward/.

Shakespeare, William. 1992. *The Tragedy of Hamlet, Prince of Denmark*. New Folger's ed. New York: Washington Square Press/Pocket Books.

CHAPTER NINETEEN

Burning Man. 2022. "What Is Burning Man? About Us: Glossary." Burning Man Project. Accessed October 17, 2022. https://burningman.org/about/about-us/glossary/.

Burning Man. 2022. "What Is Burning Man? The 10 Principles of Burning Man." Burning Man Project. Accessed October 17, 2022. https://burningman.org/about/10-principles/.

Ueshiba, Morihei. 2002. *The Art of Peace*. Translated by John Stevens. Boston, MA: Shambhala Publications.

CHAPTER TWENTY-ONE

Rudolph, Maya. 2012. "Maya Rudolph: The Fresh Air." Interview by Terry Gross. *Fresh Air* (March 8, 2012). https://www.npr.org/2012/03/08/148157572/maya-rudolph-the-fresh-air-interview.

CHAPTER TWENTY-TWO

Ebert, Robert. 2010. "Cannes #7: A Campaign for Real Movies." *Robert Ebert Journal* (blog). May 19, 2010. https://www.rogerebert.com/roger-ebert/cannes-7-a-campaign-for-real-movies.

Hughes, John, director. 1986. *Ferris Bueller's Day Off.* Paramount Pictures Corp. 01:34. DVD.

Shvili, Jason. 2021. "The Poorest States in Mexico." *Economics Article* (blog). January 11, 2021. https://www.worldatlas.com/articles/the-poorest-states-in-mexico.html (accessed October 18, 2022).

Inchauste, Gabriela. 2020. "Poverty & Equity Brief, Latin America & the Caribbean: Mexico." *WorldBank.* April 2020. https://databankfiles.worldbank.org/data/download/poverty/33EF03BB-9722-4AE2-ABC7-AA2972D68AFE/Global_POVEQ_MEX.pdf (accessed October 18, 2022).

CHAPTER TWENTY-THREE

Giudice, Maria. 2016. "How Creators Can Become Company Leaders, Poornima Vijayshanker & Maria Giudice." San

Francisco, CA. February 17, 2016. 36:27. https://www.youtube.com/watch?v=3gKyKl47xms.

Kabat-Zinn, Jon. 1994. *Wherever You Go, There You Are, Mindfulness Meditation in Everyday Life.* New Your, NY: Hachette Books.

Shaw, George Bernard. 1887. *An Unsocial Socialist.* London: Swan Sonnenschein, Lowrey & Co.

Winter Ph.D., Eyal. 2016. "Why is it Hard to Live for the Moment." *Feeling Smart* (blog), *Psychology Today.* September 19, 2016. https://www.psychologytoday.com/us/blog/feeling-smart/201609/why-is-it-hard-live-the-moment.

CHAPTER TWENTY-FOUR

Brownson, JeanMarie. 1994. "Oaxaca's History is Linked to its Lucious Chocolate." *Chicago Tribune.* February 17, 1994. https://www.chicagotribune.com/news/ct-xpm-1994-02-17-9402170093-story.html.

Parent, Marc. 2002. *Believing It All: What My Children Taught Me About Trout Fishing, Jelly Toast, and Life.* Boston, MA: Little, Brown, and Company.

Made in the USA
Middletown, DE
12 November 2023